Journey into the Light

A True Story of Death and New Life

Carol Quintana

WestBow
PRESS

Copyright © 2012 Carol Quintana.

All rights reserved. No part of this book may be used or reproduced by any means, graphic, electronic, or mechanical, including photocopying, recording, taping or by any information storage retrieval system without the written permission of the publisher except in the case of brief quotations embodied in critical articles and reviews.

ISBN: 978-1-4497-2197-8 (sc)
ISBN: 978-1-4497-2196-1 (e)
ISBN: 978-1-4497-2199-2 (hc)

Library of Congress Control Number: 2011912197

WestBow Press books may be ordered through booksellers or by contacting:

WestBow Press
A Division of Thomas Nelson
1663 Liberty Drive
Bloomington, IN 47403
www.westbowpress.com
1-(866) 928-1240

Because of the dynamic nature of the Internet, any web addresses or links contained in this book may have changed since publication and may no longer be valid. The views expressed in this work are solely those of the author and do not necessarily reflect the views of the publisher, and the publisher hereby disclaims any responsibility for them.

Any people depicted in stock imagery provided by Thinkstock are models, and such images are being used for illustrative purposes only.

Certain stock imagery © Thinkstock.

Printed in the United States of America

WestBow Press rev. date: 01/30/2012

Comments of readers of "Journey into the Light"

To read "Journey into the Light" is to be introduced to many experiences that the average person knows little about. It is interesting to see how God has worked in her life through miracles, and given her victory through many trials. Reading this will give you an insight into the power of prayer, and the working of the Holy Spirit because of the atonement accomplished through Jesus.

"Journey into the Light" is one filled with history, heritage, humor and hope. Hope found only in our Lord Jesus Christ. As I took this journey with her it was evident how the Lord had His hand in her life as he does in each of our lives. It reminds me that he gives us our hearts desires but in His timing. One of my favorite parts was the memories and journey of that special "John" that was brought into her life. The Word of God is a powerful one, essential gift that we unwrap far too less. Carol's book travels us in and out of His Word and her prayer life that is a testimony of God's love, faithfulness & favor.

After reading "Journey into the Light" I found that it is an eye opening book for the disbelievers. It truly makes you stop and think about life thereafter. The adventure from adulthood and beyond made it an interesting true life spiritual journey. I would recommend this book for the youth to make better spiritual choices. For the parents and grand-parents, this book would help guide their youth, down the right path. It would help any adult with their own spiritual growth or renewal in their faith.

I am enjoying being part of this project. … It is a really good read! Pat Crane

The story "Journey into the Light" reinforces my faith. This story helps restores my faith that there is life after death. Carol's experience in the Light is an amazing journey. She was, at the time of her death, someone that never read the Bible. After her experience she had the ability to quote the Word of God. She is able to share her experience with the Word of God. And the Word of God backs up that experience. As the author states, "God is good!

After an experience like Carol had, how could she not believe in an afterlife? She experienced more spiritual experiences than any average person that I know. I would love to see an angel. I would love to experience a healing from God. Truly Carol, you have been blessed. I will share this book with a friend and pass on His love.

Journey into the Light

Journey into the Light

A true story of death and new life
By: Carol Quintana

Edited By: Bridgette Tojek, Angelina Yellams & Pat Crane

Thanks to Bridgette to help me get started. Thanks to Angelina for the proper order of the layout. And most of all to my super great new girlfriend Pat Crane that worked so hard on the spelling and paragraphing. I love you so much for that. Pat, you are one special lady. I am proud to call you my friend.

Thank you girls!

Just a little note from the author. This book is not written by the hand of God or the Holy Spirit. Inspired yes. This is the work of just one of His servants that stepped out of her comfort zone. I did the best that I could with my limited education in the English language. All that God expects from you or me is to do the best that you can with what you have. If you find any errors and you will, forgive me in advance. In His Love, Carol Q.

DEDICATED

This book is dedicated to the Word, the Truth and the Light of this world: our Lord and Savior Jesus Christ. He died on the cross for our sins. It is His Word that I try to live by - one day at a time. Every book, even my true story, should be read by asking for the guidance of the Holy Spirit. Everything I share should line up with the Word of God; our Holy Bible is our guide. Every book is up for interpretation. When reading the Bible, always pray first and ask for guidance from the Holy Spirit. The Word of God, The Bible is and will always be the truth. His word never changes.

To the Bliss Volunteer Fire Department in New York, especially Joe Kushnor: the Fire Chief who is keeping the department going today. Also to Fire Chief Dick Maher who ran a good department in 1970, and the four volunteers who came out that night, Gail Barber, Dale Reynolds, Arthur Cartwright and Carol Roche. To them I give thanks for saving my life and my leg.

To my children, who endured and stayed by my side in the hard times and the good times. Bridgette A. Tojek, Richard

A. Tojek, Steven A. Tojek, and David Paul: my little angel that did not stay in this world for very long.

To my only true love, my husband, John, who made me a bride again in the year 2005. After 43 years he returned into my life.

God is good!

Preface

After my death I was able to see things much more clearly. There is much to say after being touched by the Love of God and I want to assure all who read this book that there truly is life after death. In this book, I talk about my salvation, my relationship with Jesus and most of all, the multitude of Love that exists. I share some mysteries that are not mysteries any more. I am here today because of God's love. Included in this book are many experiences that will illustrate the closeness of God's Love. Death is very close, just one heartbeat away, and salvation is available just for the asking.

God is good!

Special Thanks To

Special thanks to my husband John P. Quintana. His support made this book possible. John believed that I could put my experience on paper. With his help and patience, I was able to put these words into action. All of his great cooking sustained us through this adventure as I sat at the keyboard working on this book. Thank you from your loving wife and bride, Carol Ann. I truly love you.

God is good!

My mother Charlotte and Father Ted B. Czosnyka made sure that I received a Christian upbringing.

My Catholic School, Saint Barbara's and Sister Superior that made sure I was educated in the love of Jesus.

My children: Bridgette, Richard and Steven who keep the faith. My beliefs that I passed on to my children are "First God, then Country and Family." I made sure they knew that order. All my children believe in our Lord Jesus and I give thanks to God for that.

My sisters Diane, Elaine, Charlene and my brother Ted… for just being there, growing up in the same home while sharing many of the same growing experiences.

My friends, (good friends are truly a gift from God) who love me just as I am with all my flaws. Especially Denise, whom we lost to cancer - God Bless you, I miss you so much … Albert & Marylyn, Alice, Beverly & Vito, Connie, Diane, Germaine, Grace, Janet, Linda, Lorraine, Margaret, Meryll, Millie, Rita, Pat, Sandy, Cousins Sandy and Susie, Sheilah, Sal & Carol and Virginia my match maker. I want to thank God for having all these good friends in my life for the last 40 and 55 years. To Albert & Marylyn thank you for your help and being a great neighbor for the last nine years.

I give thanks to Della, for her help in telling the story of Father Baker. And last, Audrey & Mary for sharing with me my first book of inspiration.

Thank you to Literacy West NY, Inc. Located in Belmont, NY in Allegany County. Thank you for your time, lessons, coaching and encouragement. Your help was greatly appreciated and necessary.

In His Love, Carol

Table of Contents

Preface xiii
Special Thanks To xv
Chapter 1: He Knew Me before I was in My Mother's Womb. 1
Chapter 2: My Childhood 6
Chapter 3: My Early Christian Values 21
Chapter 4: Friends, Fun and Games 32
Chapter 5: The Family Farm 39
Chapter 6: Growing Up 52
Chapter 7: Married Life 61
Chapter 8: The Accident 67
Chapter 9: Instantly, I was in Spirit 71
Chapter 10: Beyond the Veil 75
Chapter 11: Facing Reality 79
Chapter 12: Family 85
Chapter 13: Darkness 88
Chapter 14: Saved 92
Chapter 15: Spirit Filled 96
Chapter 16: Signs and Wonders 102

Chapter 17:	Happily Ever After 109
Epilogue:	 118
Angels or Demons! "What Say You?" 129
Chapter 1:	My Childhood Dream! 131
Chapter 2:	The Tractor with a Piggy Back Hay Wagon! 139
Chapter 3:	The Blizzard of 1977 145
Chapter 4:	Let The Blind See! 155
Chapter 5:	The Most Unforgivable Horseback Ride! 159
Chapter 6:	The Light Bulb! 164
Chapter 7:	The Charismatic Conferences of the World! 169
Chapter 8:	My Daughter's Accident, Face down in the Fire! 177
Chapter 9:	The Cemetery Stones! 184
Chapter 10:	I'm Just A Little Tea Pot! 188
Chapter 11:	Do You Need a New Appliance? 193
Chapter 12:	Angels or Demons at the Kitchen Table! .197
Chapter 13:	The Car Drive Over & Over! 203
Chapter 14:	Her Name Was Susanna! 208
Chapter 15:	Phone Prayer! 212
Chapter 16:	Please Bless Our Home! 216
Chapter 17:	Elvis is in the Building! 222
Chapter 18:	In God We Trust 228
Chapter 19:	Bev's Faith Conquered Evil! 232

Chapter 1:

He Knew Me before I was in My Mother's Womb.

My life as Carol Ann Czosnyka began on June 19, 1946. I was born to a Polish Catholic mother and father in the small city of Lackawanna, NY. Our neighbor city was Buffalo. Western New York has rightfully earned the reputation for excessive cold and snowy drifts due to lake effect in the winters. I have lived through a few notable storms: the great ice storm of 1976, the blizzard of 1977, and the October ice storm in 2006.

According to the Bible, God handpicked my parents. The New American Standard Bible states:

Psalms 139; 13 ..."*For You formed my inward parts; You wove me in my mother's womb.*"

Jeremiah 1:5 ..."*Before I formed you in the womb I knew you, and before you were born I consecrated you; I have appointed you a prophet to the nations.*"

This is not saying that you are locked into the faith you were born into. For myself I believe I can do Gods work better in the place God chose for me. I believe this is the place most Christians, not all, can do the best work for God.

Many have to choose another Christian denomination due to a marriage partner. Other people change for many reasons. My friends' brother Steven and wife Alice changed their faith very early in their years of marriage. They reached out to the poor, the hungry, the homeless, addicts and prostitutes. They started a non denominational Christian church in a neighborhood where no others would go. He led thousands of people, young and old, to salvation. These were people that other Christians would not talk to, he invited them into his church. That was the direction in which the Lord led them.

New Living Translation
Mark 2:17 … *When Jesus heard this, he told them, "Healthy people don't need a doctor – sick people do. I have come to call not those who think they are righteous, but those who know they are sinners."*

Today he has a huge congregation and is still sharing the salvation message to all that ask. God did bless him for all his hard work. Today he also has a TV program. God will choose your heritage that is best for you. You have to make the choices in life what to do with what God gives you. It is all about your free will and being able to hear the Lord when he speaks to you. Today I am still a Catholic and share the word with whom so ever. It was and is my free will to choose what to do in my life. I choose to stay where God placed me and pray I do my best for Him.

Journey into the Light

I was always proud to say I am 100% Polish. Every one of my grandparents came from Poland. One reason I have always been proud of my family is because my father and his family helped build Saint Barbara's Church. My dad was the electrical engineer and supervisor for the city. Being an electrician, he did much of the electrical work in the school and church. There was a large stained glass window in the church with my maiden name Czosnyka on it, donated by my grandfather. I say was, because the church was taken down the summer of 2011. But there was more to my family legacy than just a stained glass window.

My paternal grandparents seized the opportunity to come to America from Poland and became entrepreneurs. Sadly, I never had the chance to know my dad's parents, but I have seen the things they have done. The AC Theater was located on the corner of Electric and Kirby; it was the first theater in Lackawanna. It was constructed by my father's dad, Anthony. AC stood for Anthony Czosnyka.

This theater has been gone for many years. I wish I had had the opportunity to witness the silent movies and listen to the piano play. My uncle Brownie played the piano to the beat of the white bouncing ball on the screen that guided the audience through reading the words of the silent movies. My two Aunts, both were named Mary, (one was married to Uncle Brownie, the other, my dad's sister, remained single) also became part of the family enterprise. They worked at the first hardware store which had been constructed by my Grandfather Anthony, and later, became the owners of AC Electric Hardware on Electric Ave. With the first church, the first hardware store and first theater, we had the beginning of a city.

A large Polish population started to grow in the steel city along with the Irish. Most of the parishioners at Our Lady of Victory were children from parents or grandparents that had come from Ireland. All nationalities attended, but its early beginnings started due to Father Baker and the Irish community. As I grew a little older, I noticed the popularity of the ethnic jokes, mostly Polish jokes. In my neighborhood, I heard all the Polish jokes and they were popular for over twenty years. I told myself that when I had children, I would give those children French names or nick-names so they would not have to deal with all the dumb Polish jokes unless they chose to. I always had a few ethnic jokes up my sleeve so I could return the pleasure.

The neighbors on my side of the bridge were mostly Irish and Polish. On the other side of the bridge, the first ward, the general population consisted of African-American, Spanish, Italian, and Arabic. When I was a young girl, the city was mostly Catholic, but the ethnic population and people's faith started to change drastically in the city of Lackawanna during the late 1980's.

Today the first ward is mostly Arabic. Unfortunately, the city of Lackawanna is now best known as the home of the "Lackawanna Six." This was a group of six American citizens who were trained in Afghanistan by al-Qaeda terrorists. They were eventually arrested.

A group of seven men in Lackawanna, near Buffalo, New York, are influenced by religious discussions with two al-Qaeda operatives. All of the men are US citizens. They tell friends they are merely going to Pakistan for religious instruction. The men travel separately and attend a six-week long weapons course at the Al Farooq camp. Some of them meet Osama bin Laden in Kandahar and they all hear him give a speech. However, most of them apparently think they are in over their heads and find excuses to cut their basic training course short and return home. The six who return show little to no evidence of any al-Qaeda plotting in the following months. The seventh man, however, becomes committed and stays overseas with al-Qaeda. The six who return will later be arrested and dubbed an al-Qaeda cell known as the "Lackawanna Six."

Chapter 2:

My Childhood

When I was growing up, my home was next to the Bethel Presbyterian Church. It always seemed so strange and confusing to me for the pastor to be called a pastor and not a priest or father. Unlike a priest, the pastor next door had a wife and children; but still, my dad said they were both men of God. I always wanted to walk inside the pastor's church, but I did not dare. I was always afraid that I would get into trouble, and I did not want to take that chance.

Also near my home was the Our Lady of Victory Basilica, a large Irish populated church built by Father Baker with his many donations. The donations came in from all over the world. This church is the second largest Basilica in the world and it is absolutely beautiful. In the late 1800's Father Baker started to build a small home for orphan boys. There was a great need for a boys' home, and he had the responsibility to care for them all, in the early beginnings, on donations from others. Father Baker built a huge church in honor of the Lords' Blessed Mother, Mary. This Basilica was all paid for before it was finished by the money of these donations.

With the same funds, Father Baker was also able to build a huge boys' home, an unwed mothers' home, a hospital and a school. Again, all of it was paid for from the money received from donations.

In the late 1880s, Buffalo was beginning to harness the power of natural gas. Pools of this efficient and clean resource were being found in several sites by local drillers and the idea of not having to pay any more lighting and heating bills appealed much to Father Baker. After persuading the Bishop of Buffalo to give him a $2,000 donation, the humble priest gathered a group of Pennsylvania drillers to Limestone Hill. At the conclusion of afternoon Mass, Father Baker led a procession of parishioners down his usual "prayer path". When he was done walking, Father Baker took out a small statue of Our Lady of Victory, reached down and buried it in the ground. He instructed the drillers to begin their work in that very spot. Hesitantly, and with much skepticism, the workmen began their task. One day, the project's foreman came to the humble priest and pleaded with him to give up the search for gas. Most natural gas wells were found at a depth of 600 feet, he explained, while the Limestone Hill drillers had already passed the 800-, 900-, and 1,000-foot marks. Unconcerned, Father Baker told the man to have faith and continue on.

Finally, on August 22, 1891, at the unheard-of depth of 1,137 feet, gas was struck. Victoria Well, as Father Baker had named it, spouted gas and flame into the air for many hours, causing a most spectacular scene. No one was more pleased than Father Baker, for his patroness had smiled on him once more. To this day, more than 100 years later, Victoria Well continues to provide natural gas to some of the buildings that make up the OLV Institutions -- an incredible feat considering that most natural gas wells dry up after just a few years.

With the natural gas found, due to Father Baker prayers and drillers from PA, on the church's property all the buildings have free heat. Talk about energy efficient! It just doesn't get much better than this.

God is good!

I have a brief story to share about the many problems that this one humble man was able to overcome with his faith, prayers and the love of God. He also had faith in all the ladies that joined his organization. Father Bakers' little story makes me believe he was the first man to believe in the power of the woman. Father might have started "Women's Lib" so to speak. If you want the job done, call on the woman, ladies and mothers even the young girls. We can do it! I just had to put in a little of my humor. I feel that Our Lady is a very good name for the church, since it was built with the money raised from all the ladies. So it stands in honor of the Lords Mother, "Our Lady of Victory" who was victorious in the birth of Our Lord, we can also add the love of all the generous ladies, Our Lady's of Charity that gave when God called. I guess this story gives me a double meaning to Our Lady of Victory, for the name of the church.

The Homes of Charity is the evolution of a charitable enterprise which began more than 145 years ago. In the 1850's, the citizens of Buffalo, N.Y., grew increasingly concerned about the number of orphaned and abandoned children and the lack of facilities for troubled youngsters. The Limestone Hill Institutions (Limestone Hill was the name of the City of Lackawanna in the late 1800's and early 1900's), as they were known at the time, were built in 1854 and included a parish (St. Patrick's), an orphanage, and a protector for young boys. Without the luxury of today's state and federal funding, however, finances became a major concern, and within years, the institutions fell deeper into debt.

By 1882, the situation around Limestone Hill was bleak indeed. Upon his arrival in February of that year, the institutions' newest superintendent, Father Nelson Henry Baker, learned of a debt which had exceeded $56,000, and saw first-hand buildings which were in desperate need of repair. Without a word, Father Baker (once a successful businessman himself) emptied his personal savings and used his good name to keep creditors at bay for the time being. But, the humble priest knew that a long-term solution was needed if the important work being done at Limestone Hill was going to continue. Father Baker, who had begun his lifelong devotion to Our Lady of Victory after a trip to the Basilica of Notre Dame des Victories in Paris in 1874, asked his patroness for help.

His prayers were soon answered in the form of a most ingenious idea, "The Association of Our Lady of Victory." Father Baker wrote to postmasters in cities all over the country, asking for names and addresses of Catholic women who may be sympathetic to his most important cause. He then sent letters to these people, asking them to help him care for the dependent and helpless children by joining the Association for 25 cents a year. Little did the humble priest know that he had pioneered the concept of direct mail fundraising. Very quickly, his idea caught on, and in little time, the creditors had been paid in full. Shortly after, the Limestone Hill Institutions, once in desperate financial trouble, now looked to expand.

And expand they did. By the turn of the century, the number of children receiving care at the Institutions had more than tripled. Responding to news reports of infant bones being dredged out of the Erie Canal by the thousands, Father Baker embarked on a new (and controversial) project, the building of the OLV Infant Home. Once completed, the facility would provide pre-natal care and adoption services to teenage or unwed mothers. To help him accomplish this critical mission, Father Baker turned to the generous members of his Association. And they responded. In 1908, the $100,000 structure was completed and immediately filled with those in need. Within years, the Infant Home was credited with saving thousands of lives.

Although the "Multitude of the Poor" and his Association had done much good throughout the years, no one could have expected their most motivated venture to be as big a success. When a fire destroyed a majority of old St. Patrick's Church in 1916, Father Baker used the disaster as an opportunity. He unveiled plans for a wondrous European-style Basilica to be built! Before embarking on the project, however, the business-savvy priest knew he would need assistance. He wrote of his plans in the Association's newsletter, the *Annals*, and offered per-brick sponsorships for only $10. Within weeks, donations, monetary and material, flooded into Lackawanna. In 1926, the shrine was completed at a cost of over $3 million, (equivalent to about $50 million today), debt-free! In fact, the role the donors played was so prevalent in the building of the OLV Shrine that it was singled out by Pope Pius XI in his Apostolic Decree conferring the title of "Minor Basilica" to the shrine. It read: *"... there is no debt on the whole, a remarkable sign of unstinting charity, and a testimony to its faithful."*

The role played by the organization's thousands of donors continues to be a critical one to this day. Although social needs, programming and giving vehicles have changed much over the years, the need for generous souls remains. Decades ago, Father Baker recognized the importance of reaching out for assistance. Today, that act is no less important. This story tells me to be steadfast in God. Never stop trusting in God. If he wants you to get a job done, it will be done. God is true to His word. He can bless you and bless you abundantly. You cannot out-give the giver.

Every time I went to mass in that church I could see the blessings that came to the city of Lackawanna. I was able to see the young girls get help. I would see the young boys given a great education and a chance to make it in this world.

God is good.

Our Lady of Victory Basilica August 2011

I used to love attending mass at Our Lady of Victory Basilica; I enjoyed just looking at each life size statue of Jesus in the Stations of the Cross. The Stations of the Cross show the story of the Passion of Jesus from his trial to his entombment.

The Stations themselves are usually a series of fourteen pictures or sculptures depicting the following scenes: *Jesus is condemned to death, Jesus is given his cross, Jesus falls the first time, Jesus meets His Mother, Simon of Cyrene carries the cross, Veronica wipes the face of Jesus, Jesus falls the second time, Jesus meets the daughters of Jerusalem, Jesus falls the third time, Jesus is stripped of His garments, Crucifixion: Jesus is nailed to the cross, Jesus dies on the cross, Jesus' body is removed from the cross*

(Deposition or Lamentation) and Jesus is laid in the tomb and covered in incense.

In the book of Luke, Elizabeth calls out to Mary saying:

Luke 1:42 ..."*And she cried out with a loud voice and said, "Blessed are you among women, and blessed is the fruit of your womb!"*

When I think about the crucifixion, I cannot imagine any mother watching her child suffer as Jesus did. That is one time I believe Mother Mary did not feel so blessed. At the Basilica, the life size sculptures were made of imported Italian marble, vividly depicting Christ's pain and suffering. They are a sight to behold. Looking at them, I was able to feel and see the pain.

I remember many things about that church; some things left a particularly lasting impression. High on the wall, to the right side of the main entrance, is a hand painted mural of the Roman soldiers killing all the babies under the age of two during the reign of King Herod. In my mind, I can still see the horrific painting of the mothers running with babies in arms.

Matthew 2:13 ... *"After they had gone, an angel of the Lord appeared to Joseph in a dream and said, "Get up, take the child and his mother, and flee to Egypt. Stay there until I tell you, because Herod intends to search for the child and kill him."*

As a child I could not believe anyone could do such a terrible thing. Every time I looked at that painting, I could feel tears forming in my eyes. Then, I would look up at the ceiling and see all the angels in the clouds looking over all.

On the left side of the entrance was a statue of the Blessed Mother Mary, mother of Jesus, with the most beautiful background of stone and flowers for all the special occasions.

The Bible states she will be called *blessed* forever.

Luke 1: 46-55 ... *Mary responded, "Oh, how I praise the Lord. How I rejoice in God my Savior! For he took notice of his lowly servant girl, and now generation after generation forever shall call me blest of God".*

I used to go to Our Lady of Victory for Sunday mass and then run over to my family's parish at Saint Barbara's, to drop off my donation in my envelope. I did not want my parents to think I missed mass. I was a student from kindergarten to third grade at Saint Barbara's school where I would go to mass every morning before class started. Because of this, I decided that it was fair to be able to go to Our Lady of Victory on Sundays.

The Polish families in Lackawanna attended the parishes of Saint Michael's and Saint Barbara's. Across the tracks or "Back the Bridge" was Saint Hyacinth, Queen of All Saints on Ridge Road & Saint Anthony at the lower end of Ingham Ave. In the days of my youth, every Catholic Church had schools and their own order of nuns. On occasions some churches would take the younger children to see the Christmas decorations in the City of Buffalo. It was something to see.

Journey into the Light

As a child, Buffalo seemed like such a huge city. I used to love it when the time came to go clothes shopping for school and we would go to all the bargain basement stores. The deals my mother found in the bargain basement in Sattlers, 998 Broadway, saved a lot of my father's hard earned money. But it was no easy task. The Broadway Market area in Buffalo was a mad house when school was starting and at Easter time.

I learned very early that when I was in Sattlers and heard the sound of the sale horn, I had to keep my eyes open. A lady would run over to a selected bin and insert a pole into the slot on one huge square table that would have a cardboard sign reading 50% off. The sale would only last for a short time; it was similar to K-Mart's blue light specials, but much more dangerous.

When Bargain shopping, beware of little old ladies, - the type that you open the door for, or give up your seat on the bus so they can sit down. When the sale horn would sound, anything was fair. Those little old ladies would knock me over with their cane or push me with their walkers and I would go flying. If I did make it to the table with the shoes, and try to find my size, there would be only one shoe left. That never worked for me, I had two feet.

When the horn went off, all heads would turn to find the table that had the sale. The little old Polish ladies were a force to deal with. You would think these little old ladies gave birth to Hulk Hogan or The Undertaker or at least gave them the education on how to win in the WWE. Each year I would get better at the sale game and as adventurous and dangerous as it was, I loved to go. I made my mother proud many times, especially when I would find a pair of shoes, not just one. Bargain shopping was like a zoo, but the lions, tigers and bears at the zoo were much better behaved and nicer than the little old Polish ladies looking for a sale!

Every Christmas my mother and father would take the family to see AM & A's window decorations. It looked like they were made by Walt Disney himself. All the windows had falling snow with animated figures of people and animals acting out the Christmas theme. Every year the theme would be something different and it was truly a sight to be seen. When malls became the place to shop, one of the biggest losses for the city of Buffalo was AM & A's Department Store.

I started school at the age of four at Saint Barbara's on Caldwell Avenue. The church was on Ridge Road in the city of Lackawanna. We had mass every day before school started. Ridge Road was our Main Street. That year when I started school, the state of New York passed an age law and I had to spend another year in kindergarten.

When I was in first grade, I was allowed to walk to church and school by myself. Every day I would come home for lunch and then walk back to school. If school was canceled, the nuns used to send us home with little notes pinned on us to let our parents know.

One day, we were told that there was no school in the afternoon and we were all pinned with a note for our parents. Somehow, I lost the note on the way home and my mother did not believe me when I told her there was no school. She pretended to make a phone call and said "Hello, is this Saint Barbara's school? Was school canceled for this afternoon? No! I guess my Karolina (Carol) misunderstood. Yes, she will be returning to school."

So, I ate my lunch and I went back to school somewhat confused. I was sure they had said there was no school, but the front door of the school was open so I just walked in. It was dark and no one else was in the school. I walked down to the very end of the dark hallway and entered my classroom. Suddenly, behind me I heard the sound of the two huge, steel, front doors closing and locking behind me.

"Let me out!" I yelled as loudly as I could, but no one heard me. "Let me out!" I cried again, and again no one heard me. I went from classroom to classroom and tried every door that led outside. I could not find a way out. Finally, I walked up to the second floor and found a window halfway open. I pushed as hard as I could to open it completely. Next, I took off my bright yellow rain coat and boots and tossed them out the window. Then I opened my umbrella and jumped.

My umbrella didn't work like Mary Poppins'. The rain coat and boots did not soften the landing, and I hit the concrete sidewalk hard. I blacked out for a short time. A seventh grader cutting through the schoolyard found me and carried me home.

My mother took me to our family doctor and all he found was blood on my underwear. The doctor had my mother keep me in the crib to be still for two weeks just to make sure there was nothing else damaged. The blood on my underwear was a result of the loss of my hymen. "O my God", my mother said.

My mother feared for my future and had the doctor give her a statement that my broken hymen was from this fall. In those days, it was very important for a girl to be a virgin when she got married (as it still should be), and it was something that I always held dear to my heart. I wanted my husband to be proud of me and treat me with the respect that I deserved. I still cannot believe my mother had the doctor put this in writing, but she did. The nuns taught us that our future husbands should view us with esteem as if we were queens. The husbands would be able to hold up his head whenever we were out together and say, "She is, and always was, just mine". I kept my virtue for my husband; but that is another story for another chapter.

Every school day we would attend mass before we went to class. The mass was spoken in Latin & Polish. English was difficult for me to learn, because the first language in Saint Barbara's was Polish. It was also the language spoken at home. In our text books, one side of the page was in Polish and the opposite page was printed in English. So I am sure you will find mistakes in spelling, punctuation and paragraphing. I apologize in advance for any mistakes. I would do no better if I published this book in Polish.

I loved Sister Superior; she was so beautiful, sweet and so loving. I will always remember her beautiful face in her Franciscan outfit. The other kids and I would call their clothing "penguin outfits." We didn't say this out of disrespect, (maybe we did) but to clarify. Different types of nuns wore different types of habits.

I think I started Catholic School at the same time that they changed the focus of the teaching to emphasize the love of Jesus more than the fear of God. In most Catholic Schools you didn't need to learn the fear of God, the nuns did the job for Him. The nuns were like the little old Polish women when the sales were on. The nuns taught us about the Love of Jesus and the danger of making a nun angry. I even got rapped with a ruler over the knuckles a few times in the second and third grades.

I think I really loved the nuns because my father's sister was a sister. First she was Sister Bogumila, then for some reason her name was changed to Sister Adea Marie. My aunt took care of young children at a church orphanage in Buffalo. The children were allowed to stay in the home until the age of five. One of the children she took care of was my husband to be. He was a little two year old boy with blond hair and she would set his thick blond hair in Spoolies to curl it. Boys with curls were very popular back in the day. She took care of him from age two to five and always remembered him.

When the children were old enough to leave the church and the sister's care, they were sent to foster families. On the average most of the time the boys would go to farms. The farmers would benefit from their free labor and also receive money from the state to care for them. It was not a very good system. I heard many terrible stories from my husband. My Aunt Sister Adea Marie was so pleased to see Richard again after seventeen years and I enjoyed her stories about caring for him. She would have tears in her eyes and a smile of joy on her face when she would speak of all the children she cared for.

In third grade, I failed Polish reading and Polish spelling. I was so ashamed that I refused to go back to my Polish school. I put my foot down and carried on so much that my parents gave in. To public school I went. Suddenly, I was in third grade again but at the elementary public school.

Franklin School was on Franklin Avenue and it ranged from kindergarten to sixth grade. It was a little further to walk, but it was worth it for me. Every day I walked to school with Denise, and I really loved it. We would walk to school on the fence rail, over garage roofs and through backyards. We made a game out of it and had many routes to school.

I did miss some of the good friends I had made at Saint Barbara's, but I was too embarrassed to go back. Those friendships drifted away until we met again in seventh and eighth grade at Ridge Junior High. I do remember Maxine; her father was the mayor of the city when we were in school together. She lost her life in a car accident, I believe in seventh grade. Her death was a big loss to so many classmates and family. She was a very beautiful girl and very much loved by all her classmates. Then there was Janet, the only girl taller than me in class. Today I am 5' 10". I don't know where or what happened to Janet. I would love to know what she is up to these days. Is she still taller than me?

Chapter 3:

My Early Christian Values

I believe that the Ten Commandments were the most influential values I had as a child. I cannot say that I always followed them, but those were values that helped to shape my faith. They were the laws that I had to learn to follow in school. I often fell short while trying to follow these laws as I grew up. I struggled the most with these commandments, *Honor your father and your mother, you shall not steal, and you shall not give false testimony.*

I knew the Love of Jesus in my mind, but it took many years for that to travel eighteen inches to my heart. It is one thing to learn about Jesus and it is another to have a personal relationship with him. I learned about and felt the love but did not feel any relationship in that love. I had all the teachings from the time I was born. I knew the answers, the teachings of Christ, but I did not know Him in a personal way. Many blame the church for this; I say the children were not paying attention or just not interested in the Lord at such a young age. This is where the parent's job comes into the picture. Bring up your child in the way of the Lord. It is sad that so many parents left the teaching of salvation in the hands of only the church and did not enforce the teaching at home or in practice.

New International Version
Proverbs 22:6 ... *Train a child in the way he should go, and when he is old he will not turn from it.*

New Living Translation
Proverbs 22:6 ... *Direct your children onto the right path, and when they are older, they will not leave it.*

New International Version
Ephesians 6:4 ...*Fathers, do not exasperate your children; instead, bring them up in the training and instruction of the Lord.*

Deuteronomy 4:9 ... *Only be careful, and watch yourselves closely so that you do not forget the things your eyes have seen or let them slip from your heart as long as you live. Teach them to your children and to their children after them.*

Deuteronomy 11:19 ... *Teach them to your children, talking about them when you sit at home and when you walk along the road, when you lie down and when you get up.*

Many parents sent the children to church and did not participate in the mass or service with them. We wonder why there are so many problems with the children these days. Parents, get involved with your children's spiritual life. Do you want to read them a story? Try telling a story out of the Bible. If your church does not have a children's Bible study, then start one.

Ephesians 6:4 ... *Fathers, do not exasperate your children; instead, bring them up in the training and instruction of the Lord.*

Colossians 3:21 ... *Fathers, do not embitter your children, or they will become discouraged.*

I was baptized as a child, but I do not remember it. However, I do remember my First Holy Communion as if it was yesterday. I learned the teaching of the last supper and the breaking of the bread and drinking of the wine, the Holy Eucharist. Almost every Christian home had a picture of the last supper in their kitchen or their dining room. My mother still has it hanging there to this day in the kitchen. It was that photo I held in my heart and mind as I studied for that special day.

When the day came to make my First Holy Communion I looked like a little princess in my beautiful white dress and veil. I can remember feeling for the first time that I was a real member of the church, because I could partake in the consecrated elements, the bread and wine which we call the body and blood of Christ.

The Holy Eucharist is the Catholic word for the body and blood of Jesus. Some say communion, others call it the breaking of the bread. Every Christian denomination seems to have their own customs/ terminology or practices for the same activity or outcome. But, we love the same God and read the same Word.

I still have a huge photo of myself in my communion dress framed in a French provincial frame. I must say, it is an everyday reminder of the kind of person God would like me to be. What a little angel I appeared to be sitting on a little bench reading my prayer book.

Before I could make my First Holy Communion, I had to have months of preparation. I had to learn about the Eucharist, the body and blood of Jesus. I had to learn my prayers and the forgiveness prayer; the act of contrition. The act of contrition is a prayer, in the Catholic Church, that is used when a person is truly sorry for his sins. I had to go to confession and confess all my sins. I was just a little child when I had to walk into a dark confessional booth for the first time. It scared the pants off me. It was a small dark room with a closed door, cold marble floors and a small padded kneeler.

I had to kneel and confess to the priest about all the bad things I did or said. I remember telling him that I spilled the mop water and I said "O Shit!" I did not think a man like a priest had heard such a word and I had to tell him. That was a big sin and I had no idea if he was going to let me go easy or what. But in a gentle voice, the Father said "Jesus forgave you and then so do I. Go and say a good act of condition and your penance, asking Jesus to help you sin no more."

Then off I went to say my penance, by the priest's orders. I had to say ten Our Fathers and five Hail Mary's. "That was not so bad," I said to myself. "What a nice father." He should have been a little harder on me, because I learned real fast to take advantage of him. I could do bigger and better sins and get off easy. The priest was extremely lenient on me.

It all seemed like a big secret. I did not know who was behind the curtain in the confessional booth. I could not see who he was and he did not know who I was. What a silly child I was. There were usually one or two priests in the parish and they know each and every one of the members of the church by name. Yet with the wall between us and the curtain in the little open window, it was all such a big secret between me and father.

Today, confessors talk eye to eye with the priest and it is much more personal. I like that much better. I feel more accountable about what I have done or said when I have to confess with eye contact. In the Catholic Church it is mandatory that everyone go to confession twice a year. This makes everyone truly think twice about what they plan to say or do in the weeks and months to come. It keeps us in check. Jesus does not like sin – but, thank God, He loves the sinner.

In the Bible, the definition of the word used by the Catholic Church "Eucharist" is described in the books of Mark and Matthew.

Mark 14:22-24 … *While they were eating, Jesus took bread, gave thanks and broke it, and gave it to his disciples, saying, "Take it; this is my body." Then he took the cup, gave thanks and offered it to them, and they all drank from it. "This is my blood of the covenant, which is poured out for many," he said to them.*

Matthew 26:26-28 … *"eat" at the giving of the bread, and puts the personal command, "Drink ye all of it," in place of the mere statement, "and they all drank of it." He adds also of the blood that, as "poured out for many," it is "unto remission of sins*

I studied hard for my first communion. As I walked down the aisle in Church, I took receiving Jesus' body and His blood, very seriously. I knelt at the altar and Father said "This is the body and blood of Christ" and I responded, "Amen." But, it did not take more than a few hours for this little girl to turn into that little mischievous child again.

Journey into the Light

This was my big day. My mother and father went all out with a huge party in our back yard. In attendance were all my aunts and uncles, all my cousins and the twins Sandy and Susie. My parents also invited many neighbors, family friends and some of my playmates that were not fortunate to have their own party. There were about thirty to forty guests.

We had Polish sausage: smoked, fresh and raw with extra garlic. We had the czarnina, which is fresh blood duck soup. Placek, a coffee cake sort of bread, pierogi in cheese, potatoes and cabbage, golanki, stuffed cabbage and plecianks, braided sweet bread. On top of all this, we had the good old standby of hot dogs and hamburgers with the best homemade potato salad ever (made by my grandmother, who passed the recipe down to my mother, and she passed down to me). My grandmother (Babcia) made homemade apple pies. The best! If you are getting hungry, just think about the duck blood soup - that will stop you from eating.

Now I have to confess to the world what a bad little child I was that day. I have to tell you truly that it did not take more than a few hours before the devil was on my heels. It was time for me to get into some kind of trouble. I collected all the First Holy Communion cards with the money in them, and I came up with an idea.

Today, I still feel so bad for my earthly father, God bless his soul. He did so much for my party, gave me all the attention in the world, and made sure it was that special day just for me. But, the temptation came into my head and I acted on it. On that day I really shamed him badly. I cannot imagine what other people were thinking about my dad.

I knew that it was customary in the Polish community to give out silver dollars as gifts. So I snuck out of the backyard and went to around six or seven bars. It was just before dark and I would walk into the tavern's door, where the men were sitting at the bar. With my sad face and watering eyes and still in my white dress and veil I would say "Is my daddy here?" Everyone at the bar world say, "O my, you look so beautiful. Did you make your communion today?" Everyone at the bar gave me a silver dollar. I would get between four to ten silver dollars from each tavern. I was raking in the money.

God, please forgive me for that one, just in case I never asked. I must have embarrassed my dad in a hurtful way. I could just hear people talking about my dad after I left with all the silver dollars in my little hand bag. How dare he not be with his little girl on such an important day? I even went to a few Irish bars, too, and I am sure that gave them a lot to talk about. Sorry Daddy! I guess you can say my early Christian values were a little messed up at times. This is the way it is as a child, we do not think about the consequences.

Journey into the Light

The photo of this young boy is my father on his special day, the year 1919. I wonder if he did anything, that he was not proud of, on his communion day?

After Communion day was over, I was a member of God's church. I had been *Baptized* by water as a baby by the priest. I did my *First Penance* (absolutions of sin) and made my

First Holy Communion. Next, it was time to be *Confirmed*. Catholics get confirmed at the age of twelve. At that time we confirm or recognize the day we were baptized for ourselves. There really is no age requirement, - any time after twelve or the age of reason.

At the time of my confirmation, I got to meet the Bishop. At this time it was Bishop Head for the Buffalo diocese. He was a very tall man. I would guess 6' 5" or taller. When he walked into a church with his tall hat and walking stick, all eyes were on him. All dressed up in his bishop outfit he stood almost eight feet tall. Bishop Head was a sight to be seen. I would say he was one beautiful and handsome man. I also believe this man was truly called by God.

On this day, I had to walk down the center of the aisle in church. The church pews were filled with parishioners. I took my seat with my sponsor (Aunt Jean) seated behind me. I can clearly remember that I took this day very seriously. I did not want to mess up this commitment with the Lord. I did not want to repeat the same mistake that I did on my First Holy Communion day. I really did feel a lot of shame afterwards, but all I could do was confess that sin. I sure did not tell my dad.

Confirmation was the day I was to become a new creature in Christ. I had to choose a name to signify that. I took the name Rachel for my symbolic name. I used to babysit a little Spanish boy named Raymond and his older sister named Rachel. I just loved that little girl and her name.

One by one, we left our pew, walked up to the bishop, and stood in front of him at the altar. The bishop put both of his hands on my head and my sponsor Aunt Jean put her hand on my shoulder. The bishop said, "Do you denounce Satin?" I replied "Yes" "Did you ask God to forgive you from all your sins?" I replied "Yes" "Do you accept Jesus Christ as your personal savior?" I replied "Yes" "Do you recognize and accept your baptism of water?" I replied "Yes."

I was anointed with oil on my head in the sign of the cross by the bishop. Then Bishop Head, with the authority given to him, said "In His Name I pronounce you, Rachel, a new creature in Christ. Go out into the world and do His work." That day Carol Ann became Carol Ann Rachel.

Chapter 4:

Friends, Fun and Games

The 1950's and 60's were good times. Everyone had a job and there was almost no crime (unless my first best girlfriend Denise and I were up to something). We had our own little crime spree going on for ourselves. We were two tomboys who were always doing something we should not be doing. We actually considered ourselves good girls. We justified the mischief that we got into by emphasizing the bad things that we didn't do. We were both virgins when we got married and we did not like to drink or do drugs.

Denise and I have always been friends. We started our friendship from our crib days. Our parents were friends and my mother would often visit Denise's mother, Mary. I would play in the crib with Denise every visit and as we grew, we progressed to the playpen and so on. There was nothing that we did not know about each other growing up. I would share my most private thoughts with her and she would do the same with me.

We had no secrets. We were more like sisters. As a tribute

to her memory, I will not reveal *all* the trouble we got ourselves into. I will, however, share two events that could have caused us a world of trouble. Remember, we really were good girls - we just took a little too much for granted. One reason I believe we took too much for granted was because my father was the superintendent for the city and Denise's dad was an attorney. From my first confession, I never was afraid of the priest when I would confess my sins.

When we were about eleven or twelve years old, we would disguise ourselves as boys and go out with our Boy Scout knives that we purchased at the five and dime to start fights with boys. We never lost a fight and we never used the knives except once: the last fight. One day, a boy named Tom was walking on one side of Ridge Road. Tom was a nice boy and we knew him. We decided to start a fight with him. We crossed the street and I took out my knife and tried to scare him. He lifted up his hand in self-defense and I accidently cut his arm. The sight of his blood running down his arm frightened me more than anything I ever did.

I said, "Tom I am so sorry."

He did not say a word. Tom just ran home feeling like a fool because he realized that we were girls. Denise and I said that we would never carry a knife again. That was our last fight pretending to be boys. That day we realized that our game could really hurt someone.

This next experience was the biggest caper we ever pulled off. Every Wednesday, from seven to nine in the evening, the CIO union hall would have a meeting for the steel workers.

Carol Quintana

The union hall was next door to my home. Every Wednesday we would borrow a car. Remember, we never stole things, we only *borrowed*. Each week, someone would leave their keys in the car, just waiting for us. We always made sure that the cars were replaced before the meetings came to an end. One night, we borrowed a black and white 1956 Buick. In the back seat was a bag of goodies that contained chips, ice cream and Wild Turkey liquor.

The muffler was dragging, so Denise fixed it with a coat hanger. We did not want to bring attention to the police by driving a noisy car. We put one dollar of gas in the car and drove to a friend's home in Buffalo. After we finished the ice cream and chips we gave the Wild Turkey to Henry, the oldest boy in the family and drove off to return the car before the meeting let out. I understand now why Dr. Phil on TV talks about teenager's brain not being wired to think about the consequences of the things they do. We did not think about anything except having fun and getting the car back in time. As we started to pull into the parking lot of the union hall, all hell broke loose. I was never as afraid as I was that night. Five huge men yelled, "There is our car!" As soon as we heard them yelling we turned around and took a new route; to the police station to turn ourselves in. Denise was behind the wheel, as she turned around the men grabbed the back bumper. She stepped on the gas. All the men that had caught the back bumper were face down on the pavement.

We drove down the street behind my home. We got to the end of the road, put the car in park, jumped out of the car in a panic and ran as fast as we could behind the Reed's family garage and to the police station. Before we arrived at the police station, we stopped running and realized that we could still make it back to my house and get away clean.

This is me "Carol" 13 years old, my years as a tomboy and driving borrowed cars.

With this new plan, we started running again as fast as we could. We jumped over a few fences, ran up to my bedroom on the third floor and jumped into the bed, leaving the windows open. We could hear the men looking around for us and they were not saying very nice words. One statement was, "If we find them I am going to kill them."

That was the last car we borrowed (other than my father's 1957 Chevy). When I went to confession that week I detected, for the first time, a lot of anger and worry in the priest's voice. He gave me a verbal beating that I will never forget. That time in the confession booth I really made a turnaround in my faith. I learned I could not take things for granted. I could not keep on doing things and expect to be forgiven when I was not truly repentant. I decided that I had to take my faith a little more seriously. But outside in my driveway was my father's 1957 Chevy!

My poor father, I would steal his car almost every night and make sure it was back in the yard before 5 AM so he would not notice. I was only thirteen years old when I started "borrowing" the cars. I would survive on two hours of sleep a night, I never missed school! Denise and I were such dare devils. We never did anything to hurt anyone, but we did break the law. Kids just don't think things through. We were truly blessed that we did not get killed or murdered. Our guardian angels had to work overtime. Maybe God had to assign a few angels for each of us.

Denise lost her father when she was about five or six years old. Her oldest brother was in college and did not have a clue what she and I were up to. Her other brother worked at the steel plant and her older sister spent her time with my sister. Denise's mother was a young widow on a fixed income and had a lot of children to keep up with. It was not an easy life for a young woman with that many children.

Denise would always spend the night at my house when we were up to no good. She lived just two blocks down the street and we were friends since we were four months old. I sure do miss her. She went home to the arms of Abraham in the heavens at the young age of fifty-five. Denise, I miss you. Enjoy your peaceful sleep.

Despite our escapades, Denise and I both turned out pretty well. She had a great husband with two great children, a girl and a boy. She had a full life before she left us. She grew into a Christian woman and passed it on to her children. God forgave us from our youthful sins. He led her to His son and salvation. I have no doubt in my mind that she made it to heaven.

God is good!

I talk about myself as a kid and breaking the law, but by today's standards I was a saint. My crimes consisted of stealing five cent candy bars, taking my mother's cigarettes, getting change out of my father's pants, the occasional 45 record that would fall between my school books when I would visit the record store, lifting candles from church and "borrowing" my father's 1957 Chevy.

One time, I went swimming at the adult education program with my mother and my cousins Sandy, Susie and friend Rosie. We all jumped into the swimming pool, but my friends and I quickly jumped back out of the pool, dried off, dressed and off we went for a ride in my dad's 1957 Chevy. It was winter and I did not have much driving experience in the snow or ice. This night Denise was not with me. She did most of the driving when we borrowed a car. This night I was doing the driving. We were on our way back to the school when we went around a corner and slid into a car dealership's parking lot.

I hit a new Oldsmobile that was on display. To make matters worse, the owner recognized me. I just smiled and kept going to get back to school as fast as I could. We parked the car in the same place and packed up a lot of snow in front of the broken headlight on the driver's side. There was more damage than just a light, but we hid it with the snow. Then we undressed and jumped back into the pool like nothing had happened.

The next day, my mother told me. "Can you believe it? The police are trying to say that you were in an accident with your father's car! But, don't worry; I know for sure you were at school with me. I told them to check with the school if they did not believe me." The police checked with the school, who agreed that I had been swimming at the time of the accident. The owner had seen me plain as day and yet he could not prove it. I got away with another caper. I told the truth about that one after I was married and lived sixty miles away.

Remember, I was a good girl because I still had my virtue and I did not drink or do drugs. Doesn't that make everything else I did acceptable? That is how I would think. As long as I was a good girl, I could do anything else.

Chapter 5:

The Family Farm

My grandmother Kazimiera Paciorkorski (or *Babcia* I would call her in Polish) was a strong and hard working woman. She raised five children, dealt with a husband she was not happy with in her later years, and when the children were grown she purchased a farm on her own.

Her husband, my grandfather Walter Paciorkorski, was called "Butcher Boy", because he came to the US at the young age of twelve, all by himself. He became a fighter to make a living, and it was said that he would butcher whomever he fought. Maybe the fact that he worked for a butcher store on the East Side of Buffalo, New York, had something to do with that name. Either way, the name fit.

He moved to a better job when he was married to Kazimera. His job was at the waste department in the City of Lackawanna. This was on the street where they purchased their home. He made a decent income to support his family. Behind their family home lived a young man named Ted, one of thirteen children. And that man married my mother during WWII.

All of Babcia's children were married and gone from home when she purchased the farm. She could not stay in such an unhappy marriage any longer. So she took all the money she had saved for over forty years in her canning jars and purchased a farm for less than $10,000. She used her mother's maiden name to purchase the property so that Grandpa would not find her through the public records.

Once, Babcia told me about her first and only true love. She was still living in Poland between WWI and WWII when she met him. He was an American Naval sailor. He promised to write her, but she never received one letter. Her heart was broken and soon she and her family moved to America.

Many years went by and she was married and had her children when she found all the letters her first love sent to her. Her mother, my great grandmother Susana, had kept the letters from her all those years. She read the truth so many years later and cried herself to sleep many nights. Babcia never got over the betrayal from her own mother; she disliked her to the day she died. I always pray that she did forgive her mother before her last breath. To be constantly unforgiving is no way to live.

I do know that when my Babcia was a grandmother herself, this sailor found her and they spend one day talking about each other's lives. They both had found someone to marry and had children and grandchildren. The truth about the letters came out and he now knew why she never answered his letters. And life goes on.

Babcia sought to spend as much time on the farm as possible. This was her way of dealing and healing from her marriage and old memories. She purchased the farm for her son Walter and his wife Jean. This was not a hand out; Walter worked hard for his share. The family farm came into being when I was about nine or ten years old. Some of my best childhood memories took place on the farm. Babcia always had a large garden of mixed vegetables, free for the picking. She also had laying hens, and we used to love collecting the eggs. Many of the chickens ended up on the Sunday dinner table. We also had pet rabbits that went missing. Sometimes when we were having a rabbit for dinner, we were told that it was chicken. I could not imagine eating Snowball or Fluffy. I felt so badly for my poor bunnies. I did not think I could ever be a farm girl. Babcia was as much a farmer as possible while living in a city. Something like the old TV show with Eva Gabor called "Green Acres" was her dream. Living on a farm was the life she wanted without grandpa.

The farm was about sixty-five miles away from the home in Lackawanna, and away from Grandpa. There was a large house with almost three hundred acres, three chicken coops with a huge barn and a few other small outside buildings. It was once a dairy farm, and soon became one again.

Crotty Road, very dry and dusty dirt in the summer time, ran past the farm. It ran in a horseshoe shape off County Road 4. On one end lived Old Lady Smith and on the other end was Bill's Ranch with horses and dairy cows. When we visited Grandma, we were in the town of Fillmore, New York, and when we went to visit Bill we would be in Granger, New York. This was a little strange for a city girl that walked from one city block to another city block to play with friends, and on the farm I was able to walk from one town to another town.

I mostly walked to visit Bill because he had horses. Bill was the road supervisor at the time, and he kept that position for many years. I remember one day when Bill was going or coming from work he crashed into the new large blue two lane bridge. This new bridge was the pride and joy of the town at this time in history. It was the bridge that was needed to drive over the Genesee River. The river was the place to go to fish and swim. This bridge was the replacement from the old one-lane wooden bridge.

The old bridge had been an eyesore for the town and the rotting wood was making the bridge very unsafe. It was such an inconvenience for the drivers in Fillmore or any driver that had to cross. Drivers had to wait their turn and many times a tractor pulling a hay wagon, going five miles an hour or some other farm equipment would keep them waiting for several minutes. A few years after the farm was purchased, a new large blue bridge was built. It had two lanes, was made of steel, and it was a blessing for all that traveled over that river.

One day, for whatever reason, Bill hit the corner of the new bridge with his pick-up truck. The complete bridge fell and collapsed into the river. It was truly a site to be seen. Who built that bridge anyway? It was hard to believe that one pickup truck could put down a huge bridge like that, but it did. Thank God that Bill did not get hurt.

I used to love it when Bill would visit us on the farm and joke around with my mother and dad. I believed that Bill had a secret crush on my mother. She was the most beautiful woman in the family. She still looks really good as she is in her 90's.

My mother was a lot younger than my dad, and Bill was closer to her age. Bill was the catch of the town. He was a very good looking man, and many ladies tried to get him to settle down. I believe he was single up till the age of fifty or fifty-five. But he finally found a true love and took that big step to take a wife. I think he broke a lot of ladies' hearts when he finally married. He never broke my mother's heart; it was not for the taking. Mother truly loved my dad. They had their share of arguments but love always healed the problems.

On the other hand, I had this huge crush on Bill's employee named Carl. Carl worked for Bill on his farm all summer. The first time I saw him, Carl was running alongside the tractor, bailing hay with no shirt and a dark tan. Carl could pick up a bale of hay and throw it on the wagon with ease. He was a slender young boy with a flat belly and a six pack. His arms had muscles like a body builder. Working in the hot sun with drops of sweat falling down his chest, he looked like Tarzan and to an eleven year old girl just budding into a teenager; I had a crush on Carl for a few years, but he liked my sister Elaine. He drove up to the farm one day on Bill's tractor, just after supper and asked Elaine to go for a ride. My heart was broken. But when he drove over to ask her out, he was all cleaned up with a dress shirt and pants that were too short on his long arms and legs. After I had seen Carl dressed up in his Sunday's best, my Tarzan fantasy just left me. When Carl was working, getting dirty and sweaty in old ripped up jeans, he was drop dead gorgeous. But when he got all cleaned up, he was just like any other boy. I heard that he became a teacher. I also heard that he has a very large family. (Just a note: if you read this book, Carl, I just thought you were the cutest thing. I pray you have a blessed life).

Carl was not the only thing I liked that Bill had. Bill owned several horses and once he let me ride his stud horse named Big Red. I was only eleven years old the first time I saw Big Red. That horse was Bill's pride and joy. It was his stud horse for breeding and I believe for showing too. One day, Bill rode Big Red to Grandma's farm and asked me if I wanted to get on. Bill told me that Big Red usually did not allow anyone but himself to ride him, but he would hold the reins and walk him around with me on his back. So I sat on this huge horse that would let no one on him but Bill.

I looked down as I sat on the saddle and was amazed that Big Red let me ride him. After a few minutes with Bill leading the horse, he gave me the rein and showed me how to use it. Big Red let me ride and I was on him for about twenty minutes or more. Big Red was so good with me on him. Bill was amazed and I was so proud of myself.

After that, I would often walk over to Bill's farm and go into the barn and just brush Big Red. Bill never knew, but on a few occasions when Big Red was in his stall, I got on his back with no saddle and would comb his mane and put my

Journey into the Light

arms around his neck and just talk to the horse. Silly me, it was much later in life when I had horses of my own, I learned how unpredictable a stud horse could be. I was one lucky little girl that I never got hurt.

Babcia also enjoyed livestock and the farm she purchased was a dairy farm. Soon she purchased some dairy cows, when Walter purchased more. In no time Walter and Jean were running a full time dairy farm. They had a large number of hogs for their freezer and for sale. They had chickens for eggs and chicken for Sunday dinner. Jean looked after the garden, plus other farm chores. It was a lot of work always being with child and taking care of the home. It became too much for Babcia spending so much time on the farm than returning back to her husband. Plus, it took no time at all for my grandpa to find her hideaway. But, Babcia stood her ground and stayed on the farm without Grandpa as much as she could. Soon she gave an invitation to her son Walter and his beautiful wife, Jean. They would run the farm as their own.

Jean was a stunning woman and all ten of her children were almost as beautiful as her. Every girl was gorgeous and stood out with their special calibration of beauty. What can I tell you? It is in our genes. Polish women are just drop dead gorgeous. The men are cute too. But good looks don't make it easy living on a farm.

It was a very hard life running a dairy farm. Babcia wanted to leave the farm to Walter because he lost an eye in the Korean War. Jobs were hard to find with one good eye. It was a very hard life for the family. Walter and Jean gave birth to ten children and one, a son named Michael, was born with a heart problem that soon killed him. One reason Michael died was because the drive to the hospital was just too far to save him.

Jean still is as beautiful as the day she was married, maybe because of her country living. But farm life was more than she could handle with such a hard life and living with her mother-in-law. Having two women in the same kitchen never works out well. Babcia always tried to help them, but it did no good. Babcia grew up from the war and the depression and Jean grew up in the good years and they had different values. Jean the daughter-in-law experienced problems that made it difficult to get along with Grandma after so many years. Two women in one kitchen and different values would never work. Uncle Walter was always in the middle of the two.

Not a safe place to be.

My poor uncle, I pray God looks after him, and He did. Things worked out just fine for all involved. Time heals all things, so they say. Jean is as beautiful as ever and still has her health and all the children are doing just fine.

God is good.

The New International Version
Matthew 19:4 ... *"Haven't you read," he replied, "that at the beginning the Creator 'made them male and female,'*

Genesis 2:24 ... *For this reason a man will leave his father and mother and be united to his wife, and they will become one flesh.*

Matthew 19:5 ... *and said, 'For this reason a man will leave his father and mother and be united to his wife, and the two will become one flesh'*

Mark 10:7 ... *For this reason a man will leave his father and mother and be united to his wife, and the two will become one flesh.' So they are no longer two, but one.*

Ephesians 5:31... *"For this reason a man will leave his father and mother and be united to his wife, and the two will become one flesh."*

Malachi 2:15 ... *Has not [the LORD] made them one? In flesh and spirit they are his. And why one? Because he was seeking godly offspring. So guard yourself in your spirit, and do not break faith with the wife of your youth.*

All my memories of the farm were wonderful, and I am glad I still have them. The first time I went into the barn there was a long rope over a huge mountain of hay. I got on that rope and went flying into the hay over and over until a huge mouse ran out of the hay and I screamed! What other little creatures could be lurking under all that hay? Then I looked at my skin on my legs and arms and it looked like I had some kind of skin disease; or lost a fight with a porcupine. I was in throbbing, burning pain all night. Hay is not soft and fluffy. I learned a lesson that day: if you want to jump in the hay, make sure that you are fully clothed.

Then there was the time I decided to take the new calf named Blue Eyes out for a walk. I put a rope around her neck and took her out of the barn. I found out that calves do not walk like a dog on a leash, as I had thought they would. Blue

Eyes took me for an unforgettable ride. I was being dragged along up and down and around the barn on the ground. Over rocks and stones and cow plops and stickers and chicken droppings. I did not dare let go of the rope even though she was running at full speed. Finally, Blue Eyes decided to stop to eat some fresh grass on the other side of the chicken coop. It was at this time that my uncle took over and returned the calf back into the barn.

One night on the farm, my sister Elaine and I decided to take a walk into town. There were no street lights, so it was too dark to see the hands in front of your face. We finally made it to the paved road and then started down in the direction of town. We saw a huge drain pipe about four feet in diameter and I went to look inside it.

That wasn't a good idea. Inside the pipe was a wild bobcat with some pups. This cat let out a scream that made my blood curdle. My sister and I started to run as if the devil himself was after us. I still don't know why that cat did not attack or go after me - maybe because I screamed louder than her. After that, my sister and I decided to go back to the farm. We never would have made it to town. It took forever just to get to the paved road.

On our way back, we were looking up in the dark sky and we saw two flying saucers. I was sure the only thing those flying saucers could see was my sister and I and that they were coming for us. The white saucers got closer and closer, and larger and larger. Then a smaller red and a green saucer came out of the white ones. I was thinking; UFO's for sure. The next day in the local news paper it was stated that there were two unidentified air craft's refueling that night. A lot of people saw the same thing we did and it got a lot of attention, it was soon explained. Or was it? The imagination of a child is wonderful.

All my cousins lived on the farm, available for me to play with. Sometimes, when my dad was teaching me to ride the tractor, my twin cousins Sandy and Susie would come along with their parents. The more the merrier! We would have family games and cookouts. It couldn't get much better than that.

Every summer from as far back as I could remember we would drive out to the farm with bags of food to share and a case of beer and Mogen David Wine. We would go to Letchworth State Park and swim in the Genesee River with all my cousins. Marie, Debbie and Sue were my favorite to visit on the farm (At this time Diana was not yet born). Sue was just a baby herself and I used to love holding her. Sue had been born with the same heart defect as that from which her brother Michael had died. This was just one more good reason for Jean to leave the farm.

One day, Jean could not take it anymore. She called my mother to drive her into Buffalo. The arguing and nonstop hard work required to run a farm were more than she could handle. Jean left the farm to go back to the city life in Buffalo and Walter soon followed.

Soon after, my grandmother went back to her house in Lackawanna. Her husband seemed much older and quieter. He soon died from colon cancer. I only remember seeing my grandfather once. He was sitting at his kitchen table. He had had too much to drink and had a nasty mouth and he frightened me. I really cannot say much about him by my own experience, only what I have heard. But I know that my Babcia had a much better and quieter life after he passed.

The farm became lifeless. It had an empty barn and house. To me it was so sad. I loved to go to the farm. I love to see my cousins. But I did not have to work the farm and it was all fun and games with my cousins. It was hard work for Walter and Jean.

In her much later years, Babcia came to live with my mother and father. She had become diabetic and it progressed to the point of assisted living; she was not able to be left alone. I was still at home and in school when she first came to live with us in my father's house on Ridge Road in Lackawanna. It was so funny to see her hide in the bathroom to smoke a cigarette. I felt like she was a bigger kid then me at times. This was great because my mother would punish her more than me. They were good years to remember.

My Mother Charlotte, 90 years young & baby sister Eleanor.

My Mothers baby brother, my Uncle Walter and Aunt Jean. There farm gave me so many great memories. Thank you. Oct. 2010

All of my mother's children at her 90's Birthday. Carol, Diane, Charlotte, Ted, Charlene & Elaine! Oct. 2010

Chapter 6:

Growing Up

I grew up in the traditions of the church, but as I grew older I realized that living the Christian life was no easy task for a teenager. My first boyfriend was when I was in sixth grade. His name was Lenny and he lived in Tonawanda. It is amazing that I remember this, but his phone number was Park Side (PS) 7548 and he lived on Gettysburg Ave. Some things I just don't forget. My home number was Fair View (FA) 2629. I can remember that, but don't ask me what I did yesterday and expect me to remember.

Memories are great. Lenny had to ride three busses to spend any time with me. We met in Our Lady of Victory Hospital. He was visiting a friend and so was I, in the same room. I don't remember who I was visiting, but I remember Lenny. For our first date, my father took us bowling. My dad drove us to "Lucky Strike Bowling Alley" on Abbott Road. Lenny held my hand in the car. I turned all red. When my father came back to pick us up Lenny again held my hand, and this time we were walking to the car for all to see. I am sure my father just loved it, seeing me turn all red like that.

Journey into the Light

When I turned thirteen I lost interest in Lenny. I met a boy named John at a carnival by the beer tent. I did not know at the time but he was the pin setter at Lucky Strike Bowling Alley. A small world! John was shorter than me and it made me feel like a giant. But I was crazy about him anyway. He was seventeen when I met him and I told him I was sixteen years old. John pumped iron and had huge arm and neck muscles. He looked like a lifeguard. He was one good looking boy. He lived across the bridge and that made him more exciting. He was a boy from the other side of the tracks.

We went steady for only a short time because of my mother and her loud mouth. He was the first boy that gave me a love letter, and I kept it all these years. There was an old cemetery behind my house, from before the days of the civil war. John used to come over and walk in the cemetery because he loved to read the inscriptions on the old stones. One day, after walking around the cemetery and reading some of the stones, John leaned me against a huge tree and gave me a long kiss.

My mother just happened to be looking out that side of the house at that time. She opened the window and screamed out "You thirteen year old piss pot. What are you doing??? You are too young for that stuff." John said to me, "You are only thirteen?" Busted! Who would think that forty- three years later he would be my husband? I still have his photos and his love letter that I saved in my scrapbook all these years. After I was busted about my age, John moved on, but I would think about him every now and then and he did the same.

When I was seventeen years old I would go dancing with my friends Diane, Sal, Alice, Sandy and Al, at the Town Casino on Main Street in Buffalo. This was one of the dancing places of the year with live music. There was a new group on tour called The Monkey's coming to Buffalo. They were going to perform at the Town Casino and they wanted a girl to dance with the band. They hired go-go girls all the time to dance in glass booths hanging up in the air from the ceiling.

I was offered the opportunity by one of the owners to dance on stage with the band, but not just as a run of the mill go-go girl in a cage. I was to be a band dancer; as if there was any big difference. At that time in my life I did believe there was a difference and time has proved that.

The year was 1964 and the establishment offered me $6.50 an hour to dance. That was very big money then. I danced in the middle and around the horse-shoe shaped stage in front of the bar. At this time, a person had to be eighteen years old to even get into any bar or establishment that sold alcohol. I was only seventeen and they hired me to dance in a bar. I was never asked for proof of age. I looked about twenty and I was stacked, (36" / 24" / 36"). Those measurements were all the qualifications I needed other than being a good dancer.

Journey into the Light

I am a very young girl age 17 years old dancing. I had my two hour career at the Town Casino in Buffalo, NY.

I could really dance and shake my stuff. Only two others girls danced as well or better than I and that would be Sandy and Darlene. I only had one possible problem, transportation. One of the silent partners said I had nothing to worry about. If I was stuck for a ride, he would see to it that I was taken home safely. He also added that if anyone tried to bother me, he would take care of that too. How could I pass that up?

Sandy and Al, a married couple, were available to drive me home most of the time; if not I could always depend on dependable Sal. The Town Casino gave me money to buy an outfit; fish net stockings, black dance slippers, a black leotard and the white fringe to sew on to it around my hips and bust line. When I started to shake in that outfit, it looked like everything was shaking.

I worked the first day for two hours before I received an emergency phone call. It was my sister Diane, "Your father is on his way and he loaded his pistol and he is going to kill you. Someone told him you were dancing at the Casino." I got off the stage, put on my long pants over my outfit and had a long sleeve sweater to cover every bit of evidence that I might be working or dancing. But between my shoes and pants you could see the fish net, if you were looking.

I started dancing with Sandy and Al, and it was just about five minutes into dancing with my girlfriends when I felt a hard hand hit my shoulder. I turned around and it was my dad. In a flash, as promised, I was being protected. There were bouncers all over my father. I screamed out "No, don't do anything, this is my father." Then my sister's husband George jumped in before I finished my words and it was too late for George. No one laid a finger on my father but poor George got pretty banged up and lost his good watch to boot.

My father believed me when I said I was not dancing at the Casino. When he looked around and checked out the place, he figured all was good. He let me stay with my friends to dance and he took care of poor George, who had a little blood here and there. The reason my dad was so upset and ready to kill was because, not too many years before, the Town Casino had been a strip bar. My father was thinking I was taking off my clothing while dancing.

After my father left, I had to go down stairs and tell the manager I could not dance for him. I said, "You saw what just happened when my father came in and showed his badge and gun. I just cannot work for you." Then, I had the nerve to ask him for my two hour pay check. He told me to get out of the office, and that he had no plans to pay me. He pointed out to me that he had money invested in my outfit, and with my long legs no one else could use it. So I did what I always did; I put on that sad face, batted my eyes and just looked so pitiful.

The silent partner came over and asked me what the problem was. I told him that the manager would not pay me for the two hours I danced. The silent partner told me to come back down to the office in ten minutes. I did and he gave me a pay check for $12.30. "Oh, thanks so much," I said with my happy face. Off I went back up stairs and danced the night away. My poor guardian angel, he had a lot of work to do that night. And I am still alive to tell about it.

From thirteen to nineteen I had many boyfriends, but because it was so important to me to be a virgin to the man I married, those relationships did not last long. Denise and I both had those ideals. It is sad that those ideals are not important to more young men and women today.

I do have one funny story to share about one boyfriend, named Sam, who accepted me on my terms. I was out at the beach with a lot of friends. When it got dark, we all went inside the bar and started dancing. My friend Gary introduced me to his friend Sam. He was so much fun and he could make me laugh.

The night I first met him, I was wearing my very small bikini swim suit, dancing in a bar by the beach. My outfit, my dancing and the location alone, could have sent the wrong message to any young man. The hot sun made me so tired and after all the dancing I was ready to go home. Sam said he would drive me and I did not worry, because he was a good friend of Gary and Gary was going with my girlfriend Alice.

This is the funny part. I fell asleep on the drive home. All Sam knew was that I lived in Lackawanna. He drove into a private parking place where lovers would sometimes park to make out. I woke up when I felt the car stop and I thanked him and got out of the car. Sam was thinking I had to go to the bathroom and he waited, and waited and I never returned. He did not have a clue that he had driven me into my own back yard.

He sat there for some time and then went out looking for me. I was up in my bedroom fast asleep. He was thinking that he was going to get lucky that night but he lost the girl. He was left alone on lover's lane. My friends and I still laugh about that to this day.

This lover's parking lot was next to the cemetery. It was also the parking lot of the CIO Steel Workers Union. Just down the back street behind my home was a street that was referred to as the city line. It was called city line because it was the division between Buffalo and Lackawanna. On the Lackawanna side was "The Coffee Pot." This was the place many teenagers would hang out after school and later in the evening. It was at the Coffee Pot when I first met Richard.

Richard worked at the steel plant and UPS, drove a red Lincoln convertible, made good money and was very good

Journey into the Light

looking. I started dating Richard at the age of eighteen. He was twenty-three and most of our time was spent dancing. Richard was not much of a dancer, but he gave it his best.

One favorite place to dance was at Shell's Bar on Broadway in Buffalo where Charley Star sang with his band. We would also go to Jan's Candy Cane Lounge on Main Street in Buffalo and dance to Jerry Allen's band. At that time, Richard and I spent a lot of time with Sandy and Alice. They were a few years' older, married, and great dancers.

Richard could dance well to a slow dance, but when we would start a fast dance, it was a different story. He would jump up and down, flapping his arms like a flying ape. It was not a pleasant sight. But he was my boyfriend and only the slow dances were important with a boyfriend.

Dancing was something that I would not miss for any reason. I remember one time I was in the hospital with pneumonia, but I did not want to miss out on the dancing on Friday and Saturday nights. I called Sandy on the rented hospital phone and told her I would put 7-UP soda pop bottles on my window. I told her to blink the car lights at my window.

I planned to sneak out of the hospital to go dancing. I did a dry run and put cardboard between the outside stair doors so they would not lock behind me. I got all dressed up with makeup and my hair all fixed and pretended that I was sleeping for the night bed check; then out the door I went. I got back before the morning bed check. I got away with it; I pulled it off. I was a dancing fool that night and when I think back, I am lucky that I did not have a heart attack.

Then came Saturday night and I had the same plan. Would I be able to pull it off again? After the night bed check, I jumped out of bed to do the same and as I opened the door to my room, there was a gurney across it with a nurse sitting on it. "Where do you think you are going, young lady?" "Get back to bed!" I guess I did not get away with it after all. But they did not catch me the first time. So I went to the window and waved goodbye to Sandy & Al.

Sandy and Al were always the best dancing couple, no matter where we went. For my Junior Prom, I needed a date who could dance, so I borrowed Al (with Sandy's permission) and we won the dance contest and had free coke all night.

Chapter 7:

Married Life

Richard joined the Army while we were dating. He was very lucky to be stationed in Germany. In 1964, I was a senior in high school while he was serving in Germany. In the last days of December, his mother was killed by a drunk driver. Richard came home for the services and he wanted to stay with me.

It was the Christmas Holidays and Richard was in such emotional pain. I mistook pity for love and we became intimate for the first time. After the sex act was over, all I could think of was, "What is the big deal that everyone makes about sex?" My next thought was, "What if I am pregnant?" Then all the teachings I learned from the nuns, of the importance of being a virgin to the man you were to marry, started running through my head. I wanted that respect from my husband; I wanted to save myself just for him.

Richard and I were married in a last minute ceremony on New Years Eve of 1965. I feared that if we did not get married before Richard went back to Germany I might be with child and then what? I knew nothing about sex and Richard was not much more educated than me.

Richard only had a few days before he had to return to Germany. A honeymoon at this time was not in the picture. I told my mother and father that we were getting married and my mother asked, "What is the hurry or do you have to?" "No." I said, "I don't have to, we just want to." My father told me that I had the choice between a family wedding or a big honeymoon. I chose the big honeymoon. My father was not a stupid man. He remembered the cost of the two weddings he had to pay when my two older sisters had decided to marry. My dad was off the hook with me.

We had a very small Church wedding at Saint Barbara's on Ridge Road. I wore my sister Elaine's wedding dress and she wore my bridesmaid's dress. Richard was dressed in his Army uniform and his brother was the best man. About twelve people were present at the service. After church we had a nice meal at my parent's home and that was that. Not much of a wedding, but I planned a great honeymoon. We spent the first night at Travel's Lodge on Main Street in Buffalo.

That night I made myself beautiful and dressed in a red and black sexy little outfit that did not stay on for long. Suddenly, I noticed a lot of blood on the sheets. O NO! I had my period. My little friend came to visit, a gift from Mother Nature. I guess I was not having a baby from that one night stand.

I did not know what to do. I was under the impression that the blood that a woman passed was nasty stuff and if a man had sex during that time, he would get some kind of social disease. I was in bed with my husband, late at night, married only a few hours, and I called my mother.

My mother answered the phone and asked "What the hell are you doing calling me?" "Where are you?" "I am in bed with Richard." "You are in bed with your husband and you are calling your mother. Are you crazy?" I started to cry, and then my mother took me a little more seriously. "Why are you calling me?" I explained the situation. She set me straight and then said, "You are a silly girl, is there anything else?" I said, "No." "Then get off the phone and take care of your husband." The next night we went to Niagara Falls and then back home. Richard had to fly out the next day to Germany. It was then I started to plan my big honeymoon.

Richard went back to Germany and I went back to school a married woman. I decided that I would have my honeymoon in Europe and I was able to take off the month of April for an "educational tour". I was receiving allotment checks from the Army each month and I saved those checks for our honeymoon.

My farther paid for a round trip ticket to Germany and an extra $150 for an open ticket to fly anywhere anytime in free Europe.

We took advantage of that ticket. What a deal it was to get on and off any airplane whenever we decided. When we were in Paris, we experienced a total electric black-out in that city. We were staying in a military hotel with our room on the eighth floor; with no electric we had no elevator. Not having electric was not a problem; we just took a plane to another country.

When we went to Switzerland I plugged in my electric hair dryer. That was not a smart thing to do. The hotel lost their electric because of our lack of knowledge; apparently I needed to use an adaptor. Our room was full of smoke and we had to open the windows to air out that room. Soon the electric was back on. I guess that hotel had a good electric setup to fix this problem fast whenever an American would visit. I am sure we were not the first ones to do this.

The electric was not the only new experience I had while in Europe. The rooms were beautiful in all of the hotels we stayed at; they all had a tub or a shower. But, when it came to a toilet, we had to walk down the hall. The first time I went into the community floor toilet I was surprised. There was a toilet bowl like I had at home and then there was one next to it with water shooting up, like a beautiful blue water fountain. It was a very pretty looking toilet bowl, but what in the world was it for? I soon learned it was a bidet. I could not believe that a lady would share something like that. It was there for the general public to use.

Before long, our time and money was getting short. When we were in Italy, I had to call my father for more money. I was grateful the meals were included with the Italian family with whom we stayed. We were there for eleven days and every meal was a pasta dish of some kind, all delicious. I put on eleven pounds. I was gaining one pound a day, I had to get out of that place. The one problem that we had with the Italian family was using the bathtub every day when I wanted to wash. There was no shower. They kept their laundry in the tub and they had to remove it each night or morning.

This was, and still is today, a popular way for a family in Italy to earn extra money; to rent rooms to visitors. That was one of the best experiences we had in Europe, because we lived like the real Italian people did. When we received a Western Union check from my father, we flew back to Germany. My flight back to the States left from Frankfurt, Germany.

After I returned home from my honeymoon, I went back to school to graduate in June. My husband was not available for my prom, so I invited a girlfriend and a few other girls in my graduating class that were not able to bring their date also to join us. One girl had a black boyfriend and that was not acceptable in 1966, one girl's date had been in a car accident a week before and had broken his leg. We all had a good time together, and we didn't have to miss our senior prom.

Soon after the prom came my graduation. And as it turned out, my husband was back in the States because he was now "married personnel". All married personnel were able to go back state side for the last six months of service in 1966. Richard was there for my graduation, but soon had to leave for Fort Rucker, Alabama. I passed the test to work as a flight attendant with United Air Lines. Once again, we were both going in different directions.

Our different directions never came to pass. I was with child three days after graduation. I couldn't be a flight attendant in that condition. I could not go back to college to be a swimming teacher. So I went to Rucker with my husband and we had an apartment off-base.

My plans and God's plans were not the same. I had been on the birth control pill when I conceived. After that, I had four children in four years. I used every birth control that was available, and each time I found out that I was expecting again.

Chapter 8:

The Accident

One day, after we had moved back to western NY, our entire family loaded into our old blue Volkswagen van and drove out to visit my grandmother's farm. At that time, our entire family consisted of: my husband Richard, daughter Bridgette, son Richard, Tory Duke our German shepherd and a five month old unborn infant that I was carrying.

We started our drive to the farm with my husband Richard behind the wheel. From Lackawanna to Fillmore it was at least an hour and a half drive in good weather. It was a beautiful sunny afternoon when we started out. But somewhere between Erie County and Wyoming County, the weather began to change.

Still, I was not worried. I had my watch dog Tory Duke on board and my strong husband driving; there was nothing to fear. We had a full tank of gas and a huge lunch all packed for later in the day. I had a diaper bag full of more diapers than any child would need, and all was good. Little did I know that with all my preparation there are some things for which you cannot prepare. Our plans were to investigate the empty old farm house with so many good memories to see how much work and money we would have to invest for us to make it our home. By the time we arrived at the old farm house, the sky was getting dark. It was way too dark so early in the day. That should have been a clue about the change in the weather. But we still kept going with our plans. There was plenty of light to view the house.

When we arrived, the first place we investigated was the basement. It had two feet of water on the floor and the hot water tank was no longer any good. I am sure there was much to be done with the plumbing. Richard was not a handyman. His plans were to work overtime and pay someone to do the job the correct way.

The kitchen was still in good condition, but the bathroom floor was going south and all the windows needed some repair of some kind. I went up the very narrow and steep stairs to the four bedrooms where I saw hundreds of dead bugs and nasty mice droppings. The upstairs bedrooms needed Mr. Clean and friends. Every room needed drywall repair and the roof had some light shining through into the attic. It was more work than I wanted to do.

After we were finished evaluating the farm, we started to head home. This time, I was driving. Suddenly, we started to see the effects of the drastic weather change. It was one of those last blasts of snow before winter's end. The wind was blowing about 40 miles an hour and drifts of snow were as high as the country telephone poles. With the high winds, cold temperatures, ice on the roads and the darkness of night, the driver of any vehicle would be blinded.

Richard and my almost two year old son Richard were in the front seat. There were no car seats available for children at this time; or any law to have them. My son Richard was standing in the front seat between myself driving and my husband in the passenger seat. Bridgette (who was almost three years old) was lying down with Tory Duke on the back seat.

Richard and I were having a conversation about fixing up the farm. Richard suggested if we just came out on the weekends and cleaned one room at a time it would be no work at all. We could make a field trip out of it. It would be all fun and games, so to speak. We could just pack a lunch; let the kids and dogs run and play.

We were about halfway home when the winds picked up. The snow was blinding and driving was almost impossible. I took RT. 39 to Bliss and made a right turn on to RT. 362 into the little town of Bliss. Bliss is like one of those little towns from the movies back in the 50's. It looks like the town of Mayberry and Andy Griffith the sheriff could be walking around town visiting the barber, and Aunt Bea could be getting all the ladies in town to bake for the Firemen's Picnic.

Bliss had one store, one church, one of everything you need and neighbors looking after neighbors. In Bliss there is this little bridge that cars have to drive under and many times some of the town's children would do something silly to frighten the drivers, but this night no one would be out to play. It was late, dark, very cold and the windshield wipers could not keep up with the snow.

I was just approaching the Junction of 362 to RT 78. The snow was swirling and I could not see if any traffic was coming. All I remember about that moment was a bright light and the color red and I held on tight with both hands on to the steering wheel to get out of the way of what was coming.

I cried out "O My God, Help Me." That was it. That was the end of my life as I knew it. My life was changed forever; all things that I once knew were not the same. Even the way I looked at life and death changed. Nothing is as it really seems. Unless a person looks through the eyes of God they have no understanding of everything they think they know. Things can change in an instant.

Chapter 9:

Instantly, I was in Spirit

I was out of my body. My two year old son Richard, who had been standing in the middle of the front seat, went flying onto the floor of the passenger's side. It was that little space on the floor that saved my sons' life. Just before I cried out "O My God, Help Me," my husband was leaning over the front seat making sure my sleeping daughter was comfortable with Tory Duke. Suddenly, my husband and Tory Duke went flying to the back of the van.

The color red that I had seen was a red 3/4 ton pickup truck and the bright light was the head lights of that truck. The collision was head on to the driver's side. VW vans have nothing in the front of the van to protect the passengers. Fortunately, I was wearing a thick wig. At the time wigs were in fashion and a fast way to get ready to go out. The wig was full of windshield glass. My head was full of glass too, but the wig took the brunt of it and partially protected my head. The glass had to be removed and left me with a lot of thin scares and missing hair.

The engine of the truck was on my head and the steering wheel was in my stomach. The door almost took off my left leg at the knee. The driver of the truck, named Frank from Pike, was fine except that he was so worried about me. He told the State Police that there was nothing he could have done. He lost control and took all the blame; he told the police officer that came to the scene that it was his fault. He had been returning home from work and lost control. But in all reality there was no control to be had with all the weather conditions. At this point we were all in God's hands.

After the impact I was instantly in spirit. I was looking down and could see my husband holding my body, rocking me back and forth in the road. He was crying out over and over "O my God, she is dead." After serving in the Viet Nam war, as a medic in the burn treatment hospital, Richard knew death.

I have read a few stories about near death and the authors talk about a dark tunnel, but to me it was more like a funnel. Darkness was all around me and a small stream of light was beaming on my husband rocking my lifeless body at the smallest end of the funnel. My one leg was almost not attached. I was feeling no pain. I was feeling great; I was being loved and comforted, all eyes were looking at me and caring for me. I was at the same time, trying to see my children, dog, and the van.

I keep wondering where my children were. All I could see was my body in Richard's arms in the middle of the cold dark road with Richard crying out loud. As I traveled upward the end of the funnel started to close and the small light on me

Journey into the Light

in the road was getting dimmer. Soon I was all in the light. But I was still wondering about my two children. They were not with me, and I wanted my children safe.

For a moment, my thoughts turned to myself and I could see myself in Spirit in three dimensions walking up to the source of the light with a huge escort. I would say he was my guardian angel. This angel stayed by my side for about an hour, in earthly time. He was comforting me for the complete trip. For a slight moment, I felt like I was in the 1965 movie "Doctor Zhivago" entering a bright white snow white crystal castle. My angel was Omar Sharif and I was Julie Christie.

I was told that white was the absence of color, but this bright white light was like glimmering crystal on snow. It was white made from all the colors of the rainbow. It was a great burst of light flashing like a glittering diamond like color through a crystal.

I was all spirit and I could put my arm through myself and I took up no space. I was all there in living color but see-through. I felt more complete, bigger and better, but I took up no space. I was walking up as if I was on an escalator. There was no effort to the climb up to the heavens, just nice an easy feeling, full of tranquility. My companion next to me was a spiritual being; superior to humans in power and intelligence and he was there just for me. This angel was huge, if I had to guess I would say 10 feet tall or taller with huge, hard working hands.

Yep, that was my angel: I had worked him hard in my younger days. He had been put in charge of looking after me, even when I jumped out of a second story window in second grade. He had large feet with sandals and a light brown robe with a hood and a rope belt. Because of the hood I could not see his face, but it was not important. There was no communication by talking between myself and my angel. Nothing needed to be said by speaking. I just knew he was powerful, intelligent and good.

We traveled closer to the light. The closer we drew to the light, the brighter it became with the colors of the rainbow. And I knew beside me, was all love, forgiveness and caring. Soon, I could no longer see my husband rocking me and I could no longer hear him. I was totally in the light.

The light was brighter than any white you could imagine and out of the light was every color or the rainbow in pastel and more yet still bright white. It seemed as every color that God created was mixed together. No movie or any director could duplicate the brightness of the light. No human eye could look at it. It was truly the Light of God.

Chapter 10:

Beyond the Veil

Just when I thought the light could not get any brighter, it did. I was getting closer to the throne and somebody setting on the throne. The center of the throne was the source of the Light. It appeared to me as if there might be three beings sitting on one huge white throne. I believe it was God the Father, God the Son and God the Holy Spirit. All three were sitting on one throne and burst of lights flashed forth from the one true God. Behind that throne were Elders or Saints, all seated in a place of honor?

    Behind them was standing a legion of an army of angels as far as the eyes could see. All was white with a halo or aura of gold. My angel beside me was dressed the same, but his robe was now pure bright white with gold lace in the white rope belt. As I looked at my angel I saw a halo of gold around him too. I looked away from my guardian and I was in a new location. I was now standing in front of the Veil or Veils. It looked like a linen cloth made with angel hair, yet I could see clearly through it as if it was not there. It was like a light white, woven spider web with a little more twisting to it.

Between me and the throne was this kind of veil or veils of floating angel hair and I could see through as if I were looking through a very thin cloud. It was moving; it looked like a heavenly dance of white veils.

This was a place I knew I should not cross with my request. It was as if I knew without words; that if I came any further I would enter some kind of heavenly sleep in the arms of Abraham. I would be in a place that was prepared just for me and would soon be greeted by Jesus. I would enter a holy place full of joy and peace and be comforted. I learned later in the Word of God that there is a resurrection coming and then I will be able to go past those veils.

I did not see my grandmother; I did not see auntie or some lost loved one who had died before me. I was not greeted by any friends or family members. I was greeted and accepted just as I was in love by all. It was all the love of every spirit that ever was, is and shall be; and that love is part of God Himself.

I will always remember that I was escorted by an angel to the veil close to the throne with the bursting of light coming out of the one sitting on the throne. I did not enter where God himself sat. I did not believe it was my time. I went as far as I could with my angel that was assigned from God just for me.

We stopped together as if we were in a marching band in perfect harmony. At that time I spoke to God, not with my mouth but my mind. Thank God for that, because my mouth always gets me into trouble. I speak the truth all the time with no tact at all and never stop to think before I talk. I sure am glad I didn't have to open my mouth to speak to God.

I said "Please God, let me go back. I want to be with my children. No one will love my children like their natural mother." God spoke in a flash and said just one word "YES!" Just like that. When He spoke, I understood what others call a mystery. God is all Love and to me it is not a mystery to understand that at all. Because when God spoke, I felt the Love of God that lives in everyone. God's love spoke through the voices of everyone, every person the ever was and is and will be in the future spoke in one voice.

The love of God is in each and every one of us, and all were speaking in harmony when He said yes to me. When God said yes, I heard the love in everyone that ever was, is and shall be. For the one reading this experience, I say to you, I heard your voice, Thank you! I was able to look after my children and raise them in the way of God.

Hebrews 6:19 ... *This certain hope of being saved is a strong and trustworthy anchor for our souls, connecting us with God himself behind the sacred curtains/veils of heaven, where Christ has gone ahead to plead for us from his position as our High Priest, with the honor and rank of Melchizedek.*

2 Corinthians 3:16 ... *But whenever anyone turns to the Lord from his sins, then the veil is taken away. The Lord is the Spirit who gives them life, and where he is there is freedom.*

After God said yes, I gave Him my thanks instantly. I

was no longer in Spirit. I did not see myself enter my body. I did not see myself at all. I did not experience the feeling of traveling down to earth. Like a flash of lightning, I was back in my body. I am sure my angel took the trip with me.

Chapter 11:

Facing Reality

In my body again, I was hearing conversations with the people in the ambulance. I heard, "She is going to be DOA." "Don't stop, keep working on her." Then I heard the sound of a garage door opening. Next was, "We got her, we got her, she is back with us." The first thing I saw was that I was on a stretcher, being carried out of the ambulance garage into the hospital. Then I passed out. The next thing was a doctor stitching up my leg under my knee. My leg had been set by one of the volunteers when I was still in the ambulance.

Next to me was a state policeman. He said that he wanted to wait around to let me know that I was in no way at fault. He wanted to let me know that my husband and children were all checked out and just fine. My husband was taking the children home to Lackawanna and would be back for me tomorrow. The police officer was a very gentle, kind-hearted man. He worked over and above his call to duty.

He was a great comfort to me. He said, "Carol can I get you anything?" My answer was, "I sure could go for a cigarette."

He asked me, "What kind do you smoke?" I said "Winston." He said, "I will be back in a minute." As he walked out of the room, I told the doctor that I was five months pregnant and asked him about my baby.

He told me that the OGBYN doctors had checked me out and all looked good. He told me to just see my doctor when I got back home. The police officer then returned, opened the pack of cigarettes and lit up one for me and one for him. There we were smoking in the hospital as the doctor was still stitching up my leg. I am not 100% sure, but I think the doctor had a cigarette burning also. That is something that wouldn't happen in a hospital today.

After the accident, I realized I needed to see my own OGBYN. The ride home was an hour and a half, in a VW Bug and it was a rocky ride. When I arrived, I was bleeding. I went to see my OGBYN doctor and then was admitted into Mercy Hospital. The doctors told me I had to stay in bed 24/7; I was on complete bed rest to save my baby. But it didn't work. Every day I was losing too much blood from the placenta.

I had a priest visit me for a pre-birth blessing. He baptized the baby while he was still in my womb (A special mother's blessing). When I gave birth to a baby boy, I just knew that he was not going to make it. I took some water from my bedside and I baptized my son. I named him David Paul. He lived for only two hours, and I was discharged from the hospital the next day.

After David Paul died, I arranged to have my baby placed

next to his grandmother in Our Lady of Victory Cemetery. I was grieving for him and in a seriously weak mental state. The doctors told me that an autopsy was necessary. So we arranged for a closed casket funeral. When I asked if I should give the funeral director an outfit for him to dress the baby in I was told that a hankie would do.

With that statement I was put into a tormented state of mind. My emotions were all over the place. I was in tears and my mind was seeing my baby cut up into little pieces and covered with a hankie. I was grateful that a closed coffin was suggested. David was in a beautifully decorated white coffin with gold trim. That is my last memory of him. And that was a lot better than the pictures that were popping up in my mind.

When I went in for my six week check-up after David Paul's death, I was told that I was with child again. My first thought was that I was not ready for another child. I was still dealing with the loss of David Paul. I had no time to rejoice for a new child. I kept having very disturbing thoughts about this new baby: Does this child think he was going to take the place of David Paul? Did this child think I was going to love him as I had planned to love David Paul? It was as if my puppy was killed by a car so Daddy was going to buy me a new puppy and that would make all the pain go away. No! That is not going to happen.

I started to think about safe ways to eliminate this baby. Maybe I could fall down the stairs or off the bike at full speed. I thought that I will never have to tell anyone. The mind is very powerful. It was the worst nine months in my life.

My due date came and went, I visited my doctor at the ten month point and he ordered me to immediately go to the hospital to be induced. My doctor was very concerned. My mother was home and she took me to Children's Hospital in Buffalo. My husband Richard was nowhere to be found. So off we went with my mother driving a little too fast. On the way to the hospital, the police pulled her over. She explained that she was taking me in so that I could have my baby and we had an escort to the hospital.

When I arrived, my doctor was called in and they were ready for me. I asked him to tell me how long it takes for the labor to start after I got hooked up to the IV. The nurse told me it would take about half a bag. Remember, I did not want to have this baby. I was full of fear that I was going to hate my own child. My mother sat with me at the bedside. We spent the time talking and listening to the talking in the hall. One bag dripped until it was empty, then a second bag, and then a third bag.

Soon, a doctor came in to check me. He put his hand up inside to feel the situation out. Then the doctor asked if my husband could be found. He told me that he might have to make the decision to save me or the baby. Mother called the Sheriff's department to find him. He was out at my cousins Sandy's place in the woods doing a project with her husband Butch.

After leaving my room, the doctor leaned against the wall in the hallway as he fixed his charts.

Suddenly I called for him, "Doctor, Doctor come back please."

"I'll be in, in a few minutes."

"No time doctor, I am having the baby."

I heard him chuckle.

"Not possible! I just checked you and you are only three centimeters."

"Sorry to disappoint you, but the baby is coming."

He lifted the sheet and to his surprise, the baby's head was coming out. He pushed it back in and told me to hold my knees together tight till the anesthesiologist arrived. In a few seconds I was taken into another room and in the anesthesiologist gave me a spinal. I then opened my legs and in thirty seconds a son was born.

I had been so full of fear that I would hate my own child or hurt my own child that I had just refused to birth him. But the second I saw Steven, I felt a powerful instant love for him. I sure did not have any plans to die at this time in my life. I had two young children that needed me. The beautiful thing about this birth was instant love. A love you could only explain once you have been in the light.

Actually, the only bad part out of this experience was the anesthesiologist. It was Tony, one of my high school

Carol Quintana

classmates, the photographer for our senior yearbook. What a way to meet a classmate after seven or eight years: big belly, naked, with my butt up in the air, legs in stirrups and knees together. I guess God provided me with a little laughter in a time of need.

CHAPTER 12:

Family

Monday was the girls' night out for me and a few of my friends. These friends were also mothers with small children and we picked Bingo to be our "out of the house, get together" activity. After an early supper we would all bundle into one car and drive together. I was married with three small children at home. Monday was my day to run away from my duties and relax.

One rainy night, after parking the car in the parking lot at Father Baker's Bingo Hall, I was running in the dark and rain. I heard a voice asking if I knew where the bingo hall was. I did not stop, I just shouted for the person to follow me and I ran out of the rain with my friends. The little girl was behind us in a flash. I asked her if she was alone, and she nodded. I could see that she was young and pregnant. It did not take a brain surgeon to figure out she was from Father Baker's home for unwed mothers. I asked her if she wanted to join us. She said she would love to, and that she had never played bingo before. Her name was Gay, she was fifteen years old, and she began to join us on Monday nights.

Carol Quintana

At this time, I was only about twenty-five years old myself, about 10 years older than Gay. She was planning to have her child at Father Baker's unwed mothers' home. She wanted very much to keep the child. Her mother would have no part of her if she brought a baby home. Gay's mother had eleven children and did not want to add to that number. Gay's mother had divorced her Catholic husband and left the Catholic Church to become a Jehovah's Witness.

Gay's family soon began to attend the Kingdom Hall for lessons. One by one they all became members of the Jehovah Witness Church. Her brother was a minister at their hall. The problem with Gay was that she took her classes and became a member. She was accepted into the Kingdom Hall. It was soon after that, that Gay became pregnant. So, she had sinned after becoming a member and was outcast and was no longer able to speak to any member of her church, even her own brothers and sisters at home. Her family was even more upset that she went to a Catholic Church for help and that she wanted to keep this baby who was conceived in sin.

Meeting Gay was the beginning of a most unexpected friendship and the addition of two more family members. She told me that she really wanted to keep her baby. I made an agreement with her. I would take her and the baby into my home to live with me and my family for free. I would help her with the baby, but under one condition. She had to go back to school and finish her high school education.

For many weeks and weekends, I would bring Gay home with me and the family. When it came close to the delivery time, Gay had to stay at Father Baker's until the baby was born. After delivery, Gay and "Baby John Boy" came to live with my family. It was so much fun. My husband was always working and never home. I was always at home with my daughter Bridgette, and sons Richard and Steven, and Steven was only one year old. One year later, John Boy and Steven were the best of friends. All of my children loved Gay and John Boy and had no idea of the difference between them and my natural born. My children would look at Gay and John Boy as a sister and brother, and I was mother to all.

Chapter 13:

Darkness

After the accident, many strange events began to happen to me. I didn't know how to explain the things I had seen, and I started getting involved with the occult. The first thing I was introduced to was an Ouija Board. This is a game where people sit around the table and almost touch the arrow in the center of the board. The letters of the alphabet are lined up around the board along with the words Yes and No. With one or more people sitting at the table, it will spell out a message for you from the spirit world. I was giving the credit to my great grandmother (whom I had never met) each time I received a message.

When I was experimenting with these things, supernatural occurrences kept happening around my house. Our driveway was very long and steep. In the winter, no one without a four wheel drive vehicle could make it up, except for one car that kept driving up it in all kinds of weather. It was not a four wheel drive, at least it did not sound like one. I never saw it. I would hear a car driving up the drive way, over and over, but when I looked out the window nothing was there. This went on for more than a year. It was not only me that heard this. I would hear it, my babysitter, my children and my brother heard it one night and it scared him big time. Many of my friends heard it when they would visit.

It became the talk of the town. Nothing gets by anyone in a small town; things get passed on from person to person. The true reason for everyone knowing everything was to keep an eye out in case anyone needed anything. Whenever help was needed, it arrived. But the one thing that I wanted to stop arriving was that car.

I would hear it drive up the driveway and stop just feet from my garage door. The engine was never shut off. We would hear someone open the car door and walk around to the back of the car. Then in a short time we would hear someone get back into the car and close the door, engine still running. Every time I would go to the door to see who was out there. Each time I opened the door to look, there would be silence. Nothing and nobody would be there.

This happened every night, night after night. After some time it just became the norm. It is like living by train tracks. After a while, the train doesn't wake people up when it drives by at night. It was a noise that just drifted into the elements of the property.

Later, a person that lived in North Java told me that the land I purchased was owned by a young man in love with a young lady and was soon to be married. The driveway was put in by his instructions. They were going to build a log home and live happy ever after.

The bride died for some reason and he could not deal with the loss of his love. One night he drove up that driveway and got out of the car and did something to the muffler. Then the man got back into the car and he stayed there until the fumes killed him. I don't know if this was a true story or not. I did not want to follow it through. I just let it be. I said to myself, killing yourself every night must be true hell. To die every night and never to see the one you love again, that sounds like hell to me.

This was just one of many unusual experiences I had at the time. I had friends that were into astrology, reincarnation, calling on the spirits of the dead. All of them were very interesting, but for some reason, I just couldn't get deep into any of it.

One night, I was talking on the phone with a friend that was into the spirit world. She was talking to me about the car that was driving up each night and telling me that I should help that soul. She was treating me as if I was something special. She was doing a good job of it, too. She asked me if I can feel any "presence" and I said, "Yes." I was able to feel things others could not. It is true that I could tell when someone was in the room, and I would also feel the temperature change.

As I was talking to her, a vision of a woman materialized outside my living room window. She looked a bit like my sister Diane. She told me that her name was Susanna and she looked as she was from the 1800's. She looked just like I did when I was walking up to the heavens with my angel. She spoke to me in the same way my angel spoke to me. I could see myself and see through me also. This is the way Susanna looked and spoke.

My friend said to say with authority, "No harm can come to me because I will not allow it." I would do it, and it would work. I felt so strong and almighty. One night, Gay was visiting. On her way upstairs, she stopped for a moment and said, "Do you see her?" I was amazed that she saw Susanna too. I said, "Yes" Then my friend said, "OK, I am glad you see her too. I am not going crazy." Then we went off to bed as if it was an everyday occurrence.

Chapter 14:

Saved

The devil was trying to take my spiritual experience away from me and making me think it was a supernatural experience, and he was doing a good job at it. But, everyone in Java Center, Java Village, North Java, Java Lake and the Arcade area that knew me, or knew of me, was praying for me.

Little did I know at the time that I had built my home in a huge Christian area. Churches expounding the teachings of Jesus Christ were all around me. The devil did not have a chance. They were all praying for me because they knew something I did not. That something was the Word of God. The people in the town were readers of the Bible (my own little Bible belt). There were Bible studies in every town.

One of the many traps that have been set by Satan is making people believe they have power and control. People want to have control and the power to tell the future, the power to talk to the dead, the power to read the stars and so on. It is all just a trap. I thank God every night for all

Journey into the Light

those thousands of people that were praying for me to see the truth.

One night, while I was talking to my spiritualist friend on the phone she asked me to describe my death experience during the accident. I said that I had been instantly in spirit, and a bright burst of glittering light with all the colors of the rainbow was coming off someone sitting on a throne. That is as far as I got; Gay screamed out and truly scared me, "You really did see God!" I said, "Gay, what are you talking about? You scared the daylights out of me."

"I have to show you something."

Gay was so excited. I did not know what she was going to do or say and she sure did have my attention. I ended that phone call fast. She asked me if I had a Bible. I had to think, I did remember keeping one in the house because it was from a person that died many years ago, and it was something I wanted to keep in his memory.

It only took a few minutes to find the Bible. I was not a book reader. Every book report I did in my school years was from going to the movies. My reading and spelling skills are very bad. I only learned the Polish language up to the third grade, and I failed Polish spelling and reading, too. Gay grabbed the Bible out of my hands and opened it.

Revelation 4:2 ... *And instantly I was, in spirit, there in heaven and I saw oh, the glory of it! A throne and someone sitting on it! Great bursts of light flashed forth from Him as from* *a glittering diamond, or from a shining ruby and a rainbow glowing like an emerald encircled his throne.*

I had been speaking the words that were in the Bible. Up to this point, I had never picked up a Bible. I had never taken any spiritual learning into my own hands. The first book I ever read was the Bible called The Way. This Bible is easy reading for a beginner. The second book I read was The New American Standard Bible. The third book was The Living Bible. Then, I purchased a huge family Catholic Bible with the photo of the last Italian pope. It was a great study Bible; it had all the cross references to back-up or coordinate scriptures. What I most enjoyed in the big Catholic Study Bible was it had all the words spoken by Jesus written in red.

Later, my son purchased the same Bible for me, but this time it was with the Polish pope's photo inside the book. I was so proud (proud because my son Steven purchased it for me, and secondly because the pope was Polish.) I never had reading skills, but when I pick up a Bible; I have no problem reading or understanding it. Some tell me it is a gift from God or the Holy Spirit. Any way you look at it, when it is about my faith I can read it.

Reading the Bible turned me around from a supernatural person into a spiritual person. I developed a personal relationship with Jesus. Once I started reading the Word, I could not put the book down. Meanwhile, the news of the lady up on the hill playing with the Ouija Board was sent out to every church and prayer group. Thousands of Christians were praying for me. These were people that I never met or knew. Due to these prayers, I eventually made a change in my life.

I prayed about the board, and the answer was to burn it. Not an easy task. This board was made out of almost indestructible properties. I had to break it into many pieces with an ax before it would burn. It was late at night and the children were sleeping. I went outside to our burn barrel and put a can of lighter fluid on the board and prayed.

I asked that all things that were not from God be put at the foot of the cross. I bound them at the foot of the cross with the precious blood of Jesus. I asked God first to protect me and my children and all the live stock in the barn. I remembered reading in the Word about the story of the demons going into the pigs. I did not want any of that. I covered all of my property and possessions and, most of all my children and myself, in prayer before I cast out those things that were not of God. I kept praying, and for a moment I was not proud of what I said. I said, "Burn You Bastard, Burn." Then I went back to praying like a Christian should.

Finally, the board started to burn and I heard evil screaming - many voices like the voices from a horror movie. All that was missing was a little girl's head spinning around and vomiting green pea soup. It felt as if I was watching some kind of exorcism. I was not fearful, more like angry. I was angry at myself, that I had been arrogant enough to think I was so special, and to bring such an item into my home. I was also angry that I had exposed my children to such danger.

Chapter 15:

Spirit Filled

I received the Holy Spirit in God's timing. I discovered that the Word is the food for the Holy Spirit. The more I read it, the more I grew in the Spirit, the less I was of the world, and the astrology chart fit my personality less. I found out that although the enemy has a lot of control over the world I didn't have to be in partnership with him.

My real growth in the Spirit started at a Tuesday night prayer meeting. After bouncing from church to church, prayer meeting to prayer meeting at many different denominations, I found my niche at Saint Catharine in West Seneca, New York. It was an hour's drive, but worth every mile.

The church was run by Monsignor Dave and Father Leonard. It was one of the fastest growing charismatic Catholic prayer meetings in Western New York. There was a great need and hunger for Catholics to read the Bible - not from the church booklets, but directly out of the Bible. Every Sunday we heard the Gospel according to the word of God.

Until that point, I had never been encouraged to read the word of God on my own.

I can tell when a person first picks up the Bible and gets that born again experience, they better lock themselves into a closet for about two years. When it happened to me, I felt like I had found the cure for cancer and no one believed me. I got on such a Holy high that I was no earthly good to anyone. I would tuck a Bible under one arm and the Bible concordance under the other. I could not learn enough or receive the Word fast enough. I felt like a starving child in Africa. All I wanted to talk about was Jesus and the Bible and all the truths I was learning.

I started driving my family and friends crazy. So I made a pact with them, one by one. Just come with me one time to a Tuesday night prayer meeting, and I will never say Jesus or Bible to you again, unless you ask. They could not wait until Tuesday night just so they could get me to stop with the religion talk. But it worked every time. After the first Tuesday night, whoever I took could not wait until the next Tuesday night. One by one, they were all getting their own Bibles and they would be calling me to talk. It was one beautiful ministry I had for a few years. I did not realize at the time that leading people to Jesus was a gift by way of Tuesday nights at Saint Catharine's prayer meeting.

The personal testimonies that we heard at the meetings touched the hearts of each and every one that came. The music was beautiful, and everyone would give each other a holy kiss or shake hands. The room was filled with the Holy Spirit. We could truly feel the presence of the Lord.

It was one of these Tuesday night prayer meetings when my life changed forever. I made a complete turnaround. A beautiful, young, nineteen year old girl with short dark brown hair and dark brown eyes stood up and asked if we would all pray with her.

She said there was much immediate need for prayer. She stood up, so tall and slender with tears holding back in her eyes. She said that by now we all must have heard of that elderly lady who was raped and beaten almost to death in church as she was lighting a candle and in prayer. The elderly lady was 73 years old, and her attacker was a young sailor. The crime occurred in a church one block off Main Street in the city of Buffalo in the late afternoon.

Everyone nodded their heads and knew who she was talking about. It had been the news story for the past few days. The young lady said, "Well, I just want to tell you that she was my grandmother, but most of all she was also my mother. She was the lady that raised me and took care of me, and she needs our help. She is still in the hospital, but is doing fine. She will be back on her feet very soon. Until then, my grandmother and I need to ask all of you to pray for that poor young man. What kind of torment must he be in to have done such a thing? Please, let us all pray for him."

My mouth could have dropped to the floor. For the first time in my life I was speechless. All I was able to say was "God, I want you to make me be like her." I could have easily understood if she asked us to get a gun and hunt him down like a dog. But instead, she asked for prayer for him.

If that had been my mother and I knew who did the crime, I believe at the time I would have wanted to kill him. But I asked God to make me like her. So loving, forgiving, understanding that she had to forgive, let go, and let God.

It was later that night after the prayer meeting when Father Leonard asked if anyone wanted to walk up front, ask to be born again and accept the gifts of the Holy Spirit. I walked up to Father, remembering all the other times I made that walk to the altar. This time it was different. All the love and teachings that I learned from the day I was born flashed before me and when Father Leonard put his hands on me, I was slain in the spirit and everything that I had known in my head finally made it to my heart.

The Lord has blessed me with many gifts of the Holy Spirit and when the Spirit moves me, I move. Forgiveness is a must. It is so sad to see people that are suffering because they are full of anger, hate and pain due to having chosen not to forgive. They are destroying their health and their spiritual growth. This is an invitation for going to hell. No one is going to send me to hell. There is no one in this world that I would hate and allow them to send my spirit to hell, or allow them to make me physically sick. When I recognize un-forgiveness; when someone is refusing to pardon somebody for a mistake or wrongdoing, I always ask them to please close their eyes for just a few minutes and pray this prayer with me:

Is there someone in this world that you cannot love? A wrong has been done and it has been so long since you have rested? And every time you hear their name or see their haunting face, does your peace go away, and pain takes its place? It is a bitter persuasion, but the end is so sweet. Go find that person and wash their feet. Jesus forgave them before He knew you were sorry. Go do the same and the healing will flow. You can find plenty of reasons why you think you should not go, but deep inside, your spirit is crying for freedom. Will you reason away your courage or will you settle it in your heart? Go on your way and do it today, not tomorrow.

One of the gifts of the Holy Spirit is the gift of healing. I always wanted to be in that ministry, healing the sick and casting out things that are not from the Lord. If a person has hatred and un-forgiveness in their heart, they will not be able to receive healing.

Matthew 17:18 ... *Jesus rebuked him, the demon went out of him, and the boy was cured from that hour.*

Malachi 4:2 ... *But for you who fear my name, the sun of righteousness shall rise with healing in its wings. You shall go out leaping like calves from the stall.*

Acts 10:38 ... *And you know that God anointed Jesus of Nazareth with the Holy Spirit and with power. Then Jesus went around doing good and healing all who were oppressed by the devil, for God was with him.*

1 Corinthians 12:9 ...*The same Spirit gives great faith to another, and to someone else the one Spirit gives the gift of healing.*

After prayer meeting and the altar call, Father used to ask if anyone needed prayers. Many would follow Father into the prayer room. We all would lift those needs up to the Lord in prayer. I would always go in, week after week and just stand in the group of people in need. I would pray for each and every one that came up to Father Leonard. Father would put both his hands on their head and some of the elders of the church would put their hands on their shoulders with the other hand lifted to the heavens. I witnessed miracle after miracle every week. It was beautiful to see people with such faith be healed.

Matthew 9:22 ... *Jesus turned around, and when he saw her he said, "Daughter, be encouraged! Your faith has made you well." And the woman was healed at that moment.*

Luke 8:48 ... *"Daughter," he said to her, "your faith has made you well. Go in peace."*

Mark 10:52 ... *And Jesus said to him, "Go, for your faith has healed you." Instantly the man could see, and he followed Jesus down the road.*

Chapter 16:

Signs and Wonders

One night in the prayer room an elder came up to me and said, "When are you going to come up and put your hands on the sick? Don't you know God has given you this gift? The Holy Spirit told me to tell you." I was shocked and yet not surprised. This was something I had so much wanted to do. God had been leading me towards this ministry.

The next week, I fasted and prepared myself in prayer and I would say, "I pour the precious blood of Jesus over me, and I am protected by His blood." Off I went to the prayer meeting, full of the Holy Spirit to fight the evil and sickness of the world. I was in the prayer room and Father had his hands on an elderly lady, I believe she said she was 68 and had diabetes for 30 years. This was the first time I was close enough to hear the prayer request. At all the other prayer meetings I was just standing in the room in prayer. This night, I heard her request and I had my hands on her shoulder and the other hand lifted up to the heavens.

She was telling Father that she has been unable to regulate

her sugar and her sight was in danger and she was afraid. Father, with both hands on her head, started to pray. He cast out all things that are not from God the Father and asked for a healing. He then prayed in the spirit.

While Father was in prayer, I was having problems of my own. Over, and over in my head was music and singing: "I'm a little tea pot short and stout, tip me over and pour me out." I was feeling this energy flowing from the heavens into my arm that was lifted up to the heavens and through my other arm that was on her shoulder. I was feeling a warm, fast flow of energy coming from above and into this lady.

When Father was finished with his prayers, she was slain in the Spirit. Down she went, lying on the floor in peace and reassured that everything was under control. You could almost see a glow of light around her because she looked so peaceful. Before the next person came up, I took Father aside and told him that I was not able to pray. I told him that the singing and music just repeated itself over and over until he finished with his prayers. He asked me if I knew what it meant. I did not have a clue. I said, "Maybe I should not be up here with you." He said that God was speaking to me and letting me know that I was nothing more than a vessel like a tea pot. I had no power to heal. I was just the vessel that the Holy Spirit needed to do His work. I learned very fast that night that I am nothing without God. He that is within me is greater than he that is in the world. There is no gift from God that I could not do if God calls on me to do it for Him. God made it clear to me that night; I am nothing more than a teapot. The following week, the same lady came up to Father Leonard and let him know that her blood sugar was all under control. Every week her health improved more and more until her diabetes was almost nonexistent.

1 Corinthians 12:1-31 … *¹Now about spiritual gifts, brothers, I do not want you to be ignorant. ²You know that when you were pagans, somehow or other you were influenced and led astray to mute idols. ³Therefore I tell you that no one who is speaking by the Spirit of God says, "Jesus be cursed," and no one can say, "Jesus is Lord," except by the Holy Spirit. ⁴There are different kinds of gifts, but the same Spirit. ⁵There are different kinds of service, but the same Lord. ⁶There are different kinds of working, but the same God works all of them in all men. ⁷Now to each one the manifestation of the Spirit is given for the common good. ⁸To one there is given through the Spirit the* **message of wisdom,** *to another the* **message of knowledge** *by means of the same Spirit, ⁹to another* **faith** *by the same Spirit, to another* **gifts of healing** *by that one Spirit, ¹⁰to another* **miraculous powers,** *to another* **prophecy,** *to another* **distinguishing between spirits,** *to another* **speaking in different kinds of tongues,** *and to still another the* **interpretation of tongues.** *¹¹All these are the work of one and the same Spirit, and he gives them to each one, just as he determines. ¹²The body is a unit, though it is made up of many parts; and though all its parts are many, they form one body. So it is with Christ. ¹³For we were all baptized by one Spirit into one body—whether Jews or Greeks, slave or free—and we were all given the one Spirit to drink. ¹⁴Now the body is not made up of one part but of many. ¹⁵If the foot should say, "Because I am not a hand, I do not belong to the body," it would not for that reason cease to be part of the body. ¹⁶And if the ear should say, "Because I am not an eye, I do not belong to the body," it would not for that reason cease to be part of the body. ¹⁷If the whole body were an eye, where would the sense of hearing be?*

If the whole body were an ear, where would the sense of smell be? [18]But in fact God has arranged the parts in the body, every one of them, just as he wanted them to be. [19]If they were all one part, where would the body be? [20]As it is, there are many parts, but one body. [21]The eye cannot say to the hand, "I don't need you!" And the head cannot say to the feet, "I don't need you!" [22]On the contrary, those parts of the body that seem to be weaker are indispensable, [23]and the parts that we think are less honorable we treat with special honor. And the parts that are unpresentable are treated with special modesty, [24]while our presentable parts need no special treatment. But God has combined the members of the body and has given greater honor to the parts that lacked it, [25]so that there should be no division in the body, but that its parts should have equal concern for each other. [26]If one part suffers, every part suffers with it; if one part is honored, every part rejoices with it. [27]Now you are the body of Christ, and each one of you is a part of it. [28]And in the church God has appointed first of all apostles, second prophets, third teachers, then workers of miracles, also those having gifts of healing, those able to help others, those with gifts of administration, and those speaking in different kinds of tongues. [29]Are all apostles? Are all prophets? Are all teachers? Do all work miracles? [30]Do all have gifts of healing? Do all speak in tongues? Do all interpret? [31]But eagerly desire the greater gifts.

1 Corinthians 12:11 ... *But one and the same Spirit works all these things, distributing to each one individually just as He wills.*

Romans 12:6 ... *Since we have gifts that differ according to the grace given to us, each of us is to exercise them accordingly: if prophecy, according to the proportion of his faith;*

Ephesians 4:11… *And He gave some as apostles, and some as prophets, and some as evangelists, and some as pastors and teachers,*

Hebrews 2:4 … *God also testifying with them, both by signs and wonders and by various miracles and by gifts of the Holy Spirit according to His own will.*

John 4:48 … *So Jesus said to him, "Unless you people see signs and wonders, you simply will not believe."*

Every Tuesday night I learned something new and wonderful. I would then share it with the members of my church, Saint Patrick's, in Java Center. My priest at Saint Patrick's really did not like me. Actually, it was really the charismatic movement in the church that he did not like. Every week, another member would go to a Saint Catharine Tuesday night meeting and Father would get another one like me.

One by one, my little church was changing. I even became a teacher to the first grade on Monday nights at Saint Patrick's. Later, we started to bring music into my little church. To make all the members happy, Father did the 9 AM traditional mass and at the 11 AM we had the drums and guitars with the young people playing. Many of us would pray in song with our hands lifted up to the Lord.

The Christian life was something I wanted for my children too. All three of my children made their First Holy Communion at Saint Patrick's in Java Center. But they were all baptized at Saint Barbara's in Lackawanna. I made a lot of good Christian friends in the Java and Sheldon Townships.

Journey into the Light

From time to time, I would go to my friend Linda's house in Java Lake for a prayer meeting. On Thursdays, Linda's Aunt Rita would have a Bible study and prayer meeting in North Java and I would take my children. On other occasions, there would be guest speakers at Couriers Church, in Couriers Corner. My neighbor Mary and family went to this church where her son David had grown into a Christian man and became a pastor. Mary would tell me when a good speaker was coming to speak at her church. All around me were great Christian people and it was a great place to raise my children.

I hope I am not misleading when I speak about my darling little children. I never had labor pains in the delivery room. Instead, I had to suffer the growing pains as they were growing up. They were not always angels. One night, I had a friend drive my two boys into the Full Gospel to go to the Royal Rangers (similar to the Boy Scouts) and my daughter for young girls Bible Study. I soon received a call from my brother who had picked up my girl from K-Mart across from the church for shoplifting. I wonder where she got that from.

My older boy was always fighting on the school bus. He was the school bus bully. I could understand that, I was the bus bully when I was growing up too. My younger boy was neat as a pin. He would set his toys up just perfectly, and then the older children would move them around. Then they would mess up his bed or move his pillow, either of which would drive him crazy. He was Mr. Clean and could not deal with any mess or anything out of order.

Regardless of all the pain they put me through; I did not

need to worry. Raise them up in the way of the Lord and they shall not depart. It does not say they will not stray, or never sin. This is real life I am talking about. But God does give us His Word and that is perfect for me.

Proverbs 22:6 ... *Direct your children onto the right path, and when they are older, they will not leave it.*

Occasionally, I drove my children into Orchard Park to go to the Assembly of God Church with Pastor Tommy Reed. He had some great teachings and great speakers. But when it was all said and done, I always remembered my roots that God gave me. I know my roots and I can best serve where God placed me. I can get fed in many places. I can fellowship with any Christian and feel at home. We Christians use different words, we have different denominations but we still are all brothers and sisters in Christ.

Chapter 17:

Happily Ever After

My marriage started out well, but it did not last. Maybe the responsibility of so many children so fast was too much for Richard. Although Richard had many faults, he was a hard worker. I think his first love was working and making money. To make a long story short there was too many problems for us to deal with. After seventeen years our marriage was over. We had two different life styles. To be equally yoked is a must for a marriage to survive in my opinion.

As much as I did not want to divorce him because he was the father of my children, I did eventually file for divorce. Looking back, I wish I had talked more with my children sooner. They have since asked me, "Ma, what took you so long to get divorced?" All the time I was taking the abuse, I was thinking I was doing it to keep the family together for the children's sake. But my children had wanted it to end years sooner.

Today, Richard has a relationship with his children. I am very happy for that. After all, he is the father of my wonderful

Christian children. They saw his life and they saw my life and they all made the choice to choose the Christian standard of living. Children learn by example. I have to give him thanks for that. Richard lives about fifteen miles from where my current husband and I live. About once a week he stops for a short visit when he comes into the village to say "hello." On most of his visits he would bring us fresh vegetables from his garden. For the sake of all the children, it is a good thing. I am proud that Richard has become a better man. And he does realize that as he is doing well with his third family. He has fathered 10 children (three families) and all the brothers and sisters associate with each other. They get along like brothers and sisters should. God is good.

As a single mother, all I needed was a husband to look after me and be a good father to my children. One of my friends said to me that it is just as easy to fall in love with a rich man as it is a poor one. So I went searching first in the newspapers for a wonderful rich man. I placed an ad three times in The Buffalo Evening News and had hundreds of replies. My friends and I would have a great time reading the letters. Occasionally I would meet up with some of the men that replied. At first, as advised by the guidelines of the newspapers, I would meet them in a public restaurant to be safe.

Some were nice, but most of them had the same idea as I did. Let me tell you, money sticks with money. Every man that had a few dollars just wanted arm candy. I was a beautiful woman, arm candy. I knew that I was not lacking in the beauty department, just in the brains. But when I started to date more of the men that replied, I ran into some really big losers. One asked permission to change his pampers, – he had just had surgery. That was way too much information for me on a first date. One man asked for a goodnight kiss. He was shorter than I. I could see clearly that he was almost bald, he combed the little hair he had from one side to the other. If that was not bad enough, he also had a long thin pony tail with the total count of ten hairs The biggest problem was he had no teeth. I could not see myself kissing him and running my fingers through his hair. I never felt so uncomfortable in my life when I said, "No."

One of my dates led me to call the police. I lived in the country, and I had made plans to meet at an intersection in East Aurora, NY. Just down the road, about six or seven miles, was the restaurant we were to have our lunch together. As he arrived in his car I told him to just follow me. His sweet- talked me into getting into his car. That was a big mistake.

We arrived at the restaurant, and we started to order. I had a diet drink and he ordered some expensive hard liquor to drink for lunch. I would not take advantage of any date for the first time, so I ordered a salad of some kind. The date ordered the most expensive lunch with more hard liquor.

I was starting to worry about the drive back to my car. I excused myself, went to the ladies' room, and then returned to my diet drink. My salad was finished, but he was still eating and drinking. Then he excused himself to go to the men's room. After some time I asked the waiter to check the men's room for my date. He was gone for a very long time. The waiter asked me if he was driving a four door dark blue sedan. When I nodded, he told me that my date had left a few minutes before.

I could not believe he left me like that and with a very large bill to pay. Thank God I had the money to pay it. After I paid the bill in protest, I walked over to the bar. I sat down and asked the bartender if he knew the men who were sitting at the bar. The bartender told me that they were regulars. I then walked up to a few men and asked if one of them could drive me to my car. One said that it wasn't a problem, because he was going that way.

I arrived home safely, and then called the East Aurora police. I told the officer that I didn't know if this man broke any laws but I wanted to report him so he would not do this to any other young woman. This man found a good way to eat and drink for just the cost of gas. What a setup he had. He appeared to be a man of means and I was so angry that he would do something like that.

The police told me that if I hadn't paid the bill and had called them for a ride to my car they would have a case. But because I took care of the bill and arrived at my car and home safely, there was nothing they could do. I was angry and could not do a thing about it. I prayed with extra fervor that night. Oh God! Please, please, please find me a good husband and father.

I also tried to visit a few meetings of a group called "Parents without Partners." That was a great lead. I thought that some dad was out there who had a little girl that could use a mother, and I had two sons who could use a dad. I wanted someone to take them fishing or hunting or just play ball. So, off I went to my first meeting. The meeting had a lot of great ideas. A pool party with hot tub was one. Going boating on the water was another idea. The ideas that came up were from the members that had the means to provide the pool, hot tub and boats. I threw my hat in and said that I had horses, and perhaps we could invite parents whose children would enjoy the horses. Quickly, one of the members put me in my place. She told me that the members don't go on these events with the children. I was so confused. What is the point to have parents without partners without the children? I was soon informed that this unit was more like swingers in the 70's. It was all about sex!

So, I went to a meeting of a different chapter a few weeks later. When I walked into the room every man's eye was on me. Every woman was looking at me as if I was the enemy. This chapter was all about mirror, mirror on the wall, who is the most beautiful mother of us all. Not one lady would talk to me and the only welcome I received was the men taking a number to dance with me. I am sure that somewhere out there a good unit of Parents without Partners exists; I just did not find it.

My searching led me to Ladies' Night. Tuesday it was the Marriot. Thursday it was at Craw Daddy's. Any place would do on Friday and Saturday if there was music.

I had more single friends than I needed to go to the bars. If there was dancing, I was there. I found a lot of dancing partners and was offered one night stands.

Thankfully, I never fell far enough from the cross to stoop

to one night stands. At every church service I attended I would scan the left hands of the men to see if I could find any eligible bachelor. I dated a painter, dentist, engineer, contractor and a self-employed man. That was my lineup for twenty two years. How could I tell a forty or forty-five year old man that I wanted to be a virgin to the man I was going to marry. I didn't think it would work, and I didn't want to lose my boyfriends, so I complied with their wishes.

Every day for twenty-two years, I prayed the following prayer: "Lord, I do not want to die in sin. Please help me find a good husband for me and a good father for my three children. The only thing I need to make it back to the light is a good man to marry me and make me right with God. I don't want to die in sin."

The most blessed ending to my little story is that through my entire sinning and backsliding, God was still with me. God's love is everlasting. He never gives up or forgets the needs or the desires of our hearts. I like to say, "Let God be God" because I am so imperfect. I have too many needs and wants. I desired much more than what was needed. I had food, clothing and a roof over my head. I was blessed! Having a husband to love me would have just been an added bonus.

After I stopped searching for the man of my dreams, my dreams came true. Out of the blue one day, I went to visit my good friend, Virginia, in Woodlawn, NY. We have been friends since fourteen or fifteen years old. I do and always loved Virginia, we had so many young memories we shared together. Good friends are truly a treasure and another gift from God. I was asking her if she remembered John, the old boyfriend whom I had dated when I was thirteen. She informed me that his wife died from cancer last year and that he had just been visiting his sister who lived right across the street.

Virginia told me that he had just left with his son on their Harleys to head back home to Florida. I was crushed that I just missed him. As I was about to leave to return home to Buffalo, I heard the roaring sound of rubber on the road that only a Harley can make. He hadn't left yet. I felt like a teenager again. I felt like I was in the movie "Grease" and John was coming for me.

I was fifty-five years old, over-weight and far from being arm candy for any man. I had no makeup on and my hair was not fixed. I did not look my best. Yet, when he came up to the car window and looked at me there were a thousand butterflies fluttering in my belly. John had been my boyfriend when I was thirteen years old. We had drifted apart, but I never forgot him and he never forgot me. Forty-three years later, I felt the same way all over again. I told him that I would be right back; don't go anywhere. I quickly drove home and put on some makeup and a clean outfit.

I drove back and sat on his sister Audrey's porch. I met his sister and his son. I sat as close to him as possible. He just touched me and I was melting. It was love at first sight, or maybe I should say, love a second time around. He was leaving to get his son home but he took my phone number and said he was going to call and would drive back as soon as he could.

Carol Quintana

When he arrived home, my John called as he said he would. We talked for such a long time. I wanted the call to never end. I was wondering if he was ever going to come back to me. After a few days, I received a call from my John from the state of Virginia. He told me that he had to get some sleep, but he would see me tomorrow. He was returning for me. He was really coming! Star struck in love, I started to pack items that I would need in Florida.

After forty-three years, John and I met again and we were married in 2005. This was the first time I felt real love. My prayers were answered, and it was the first time I was able to love a man and feel the love back. My John allowed me to feel what it was to be a woman, to love a man, and have that man love you back. This is the kind of love the Bible speaks about. At the age of fifty five, I found out what the big deal was about sex. It comes to you when you love someone and they love you. Without love, it is not worth much. John has two children and I have three. Together we have a family of five, with eight grandchildren and one great-granddaughter. I give all the glory to God for finding true love with a great man. God is good!

Mr. & Mrs. John Quintana

**My extra three blessings from God!
"Steven, Bridgette, myself and Richard"**

Epilogue:

I married John and moved to Florida on August 1, 2005. After a few years, my sister Diane purchased the house next to me. Soon, my husband's sister Cathy purchased a home on the next street, then four friends moved in on the same street, Della & Bob, Mary and her sister-in-law Audrey.

It was a great time. We all lived in New York in the summer. When October came around, one by one we all started to drive or fly to Florida. We spent many nights playing board games and just having fun like a bunch of kids. Some nights we would talk about the Bible, and share our interpretations of the Word of God. We would have some debates and that would lead me back to open the Bible to find the correct scripture. Most of the time I knew the answer, but without the Word to back me up I felt empty.

Many times I would be in a situation where a question would be asked of me, and I would say a very short prayer in the Spirit. Next, just like that, I would speak the Word of God. The Word would come pouring out of my mouth.

My tongue would quote this and that and it would be as if I memorized every word in the Book.

Then there were many times when I had nothing to say. That does not happen too often. I am a talker and need to be told to quiet down, slow down, or just shut up. Such is my nature, and it needs to be harnessed at times.

One thing that has always been harnessed was the ability to read a book. Up until I moved to Florida, the Bible was the only book I read with understanding. I shared this with Audrey and Mary one night in conversation during a board game.

The next afternoon, Audrey came over as she was walking her new little puppy and carrying a book. She said, "Carol you need to read this book. The book is about a man that was dead for ninety minutes." I said that I could not understand what I read. My reading comprehension is really bad. Audrey stated, "Not with this story. It is easy reading." So I decided to give it a try.

I started to read the book and I could not put it down. I wanted to see if his experience with death was anything like mine. When I was finished, I shared the story with my friend Bev. Bev said if you enjoyed that book you must read *Embraced by the Light*. So, I read this book too. Again, I wanted to see if her experience was anything like mine. After reading these books, I realized I had something to share with my experience. But what amazed me the most is that I was able to read and understand what I was reading.

I learned that my reading skills had improved through the years. Or maybe God wanted me to read them so I would want to share my experience. We all have a purpose in God's kingdom. We all have a purpose in life. Each and every life is valuable to God. He wants each and everyone to be the best that they can be.

By me telling my little story I pray it helps me be a better person. I pray it leads me to have a more positive and functional life with His approval. Most of all, I pray it will help the reader. This should give every reader the desire to get back into the Word of God.

All things are possible in the Lord. Look at me, I am without the ability to publish a book, yet I am. Ask and you will receive. It is not an overnight thing getting a book published, yet here I am with my first book. God is good!

I am sure this is not the most perfect book you ever read or plan to read. It was not written by the hand of God. It was inspired by Him. It was written by one woman doing the best that she could. So to speak, Carol is doing the best that Carol can do and that is all God can expect from any of us. With all my faults, I stepped out of my comfort zone and stepped out in faith. My only hope is that you enjoyed my little story and it brings you closer to God and the desire to read more of His word. Just open the Bible and read. Don't fear the Holy Spirit. The gifts are for the asking. Give Jesus a fair chance in your life. ***Just give Jesus a fair chance.***

If you want to know God in a personal way just read these few words and accept them into your heart.

"Dear Jesus,
I am a sinner.
I repent of my sins.
Please forgive me and save me by your shed blood;
come into my heart.
I want to receive you as my own personal Lord and savior.
Amen"

In His Love, Carol.

Journey into the Light

After I married John I became a member of a new and second family. The men and women in the photos; are at John's cousins picnic in Angola, NY Aug. 2011. John's family is mostly Italian, Spanish and Mexican.

My husband John's mother's family came from Italy and his father from Spain. John lost his father at the young age of seven. John's new dad was Mexican. Let me tell you a little about my new family that I love. They are all excellent cooks, the men and women alike. Italian food, Spanish food and Mexican food all new to me. Yes, I love this family.

All of John's siblings married Polish. They are not just great sister-in-laws and brothers-in-laws but smart too. Everyone in this family has a clean home and great food. A good marriage is lucky to have a good family foundation and everyone loves each other just as we are.

I must say a little note to Judy my other sister-in-law from the Polish side. John's first wife Sue passed away at the young age of only 55 years to cancer. Judy is Sue's sister. Judy you are the one I must impress (impress is our private little joke). You are the glue of love for the family and I love you for that. Tom & Judy thank you.

If you want a best seller, marry into a large family, and add family photos into your book.

I give thanks to God for all my family and friends.

Angels or Demons!
"What Say You?"

In this chapter I will share my life before my near death or I say my death experience. I will take you on a little walk in my shoes through my life. Many simple yet remarkable experiences are the topic of this chapter. Why or for what reason did these experiences occur? Or are they the ranting of an aggressive crazy lady? Am I acting in an aggressive or bombastic way? It is up to you to decide. I tell you true, these things did transpire. Learning the source of these experiences took years of reading the Word of God. I also learned from many educated elders in these areas. But for me, it is by prayer and asking God for guidance in the Word. I wanted to educate myself about the reasons that these things happened. This I know, God wants Carol to be the best Carol that Carol can be. We all have a path in life to discern and then follow for God. It is our free will that will take us off the correct road. It is also our free will to get back on the road or path that God would like us to follow. I have been off the road more times than I would like to talk about. And I am not proud of that statement. Some things are easily explained and others not so. Some experiences took place many years before my accident. Years later I was able to see the reasons; the where and the why became clear. Study the word and come to your own conclusion.

Chapter 1

My Childhood Dream!

One of my earliest memories of a strange experience started at the age of twelve years old. After I was confirmed, or as my brothers and sisters in Christ would say "Born Again," I was having the same dream month after month and then year after year. That dream stopped after my second born was about two years old.

The dream was about me running away from a huge explosion followed by an enormous fire. I was running and pulling a little girl with my right arm. She was about three years old and had long blonde hair. In my left arm, I was holding a little blonde hair boy still in diapers. I was in a pair of designer jeans, pulling and holding the two children that I knew were mine. I kept looking back in tears and horror as if there was something more I should have with me as I was running. Yet there was nothing more that I could do. It was so very strange to me, because I was a city girl and I was on a stone road with pine trees on both sides of me. I always wore jeans, Wranglers. I had never known, seen or heard about designer jeans at that time. Yet I clearly remember thinking they were really nice jeans. So strange, I am in tears, terrified and I love my jeans. My only country experience was on my grandmother's farm, no pine trees or woods on the farm. What was I running from? Where was I? What caused the explosion and fire? The dream always started and ended the same. I never knew where I was going or where I came from. The realization came many years later as I explain in the next paragraphs.

My husband and I purchased five acres to build a home with a barn and kennel. The land was all wooded and full of pine trees. The drive way was very steep. As you ascended, it was S shaped dirt and stone drive way. At the top of the hill was a long, flat, straight drive way that leads to the place I wanted to build my barn. The barn was to be built first; the dimensions were twenty four by thirty four feet. First the barn, so I could build it just the way I wanted. Once we started to build our home, we would not have the money for the barn I dreamed of. My dream barn and kennel was to have a second floor for hay with a pull down stair case. The down stairs with the main entrance door was to be an office. The garage door was to open into three horse stalls. The dog kennel was to be thirty four feet long with storage and water supply.

After the barn was completed my husband was laid off from the steel plant. We knew that the unemployment checks would end. Needless to say, our barn and kennel was the beginning of our home. Move into it or lose it. My office became our living room. The three horse stalls became our dining room. The long dog kennel became our kitchen and bathroom. And at bed time, we would pull down the stairs and go up to our one huge bed room for all. It was called the hay loft bedroom.

As we started to make the barn our home, we had to make a few changes. One of the first things we did was to change the horse stall area into our dining room.

We nailed together some old storm windows in front of the garage door. This way we could open the garage door from the inside. We were then able to see outside through the nasty old wall of old storm windows. By this substitute, we were able to enjoy the morning sun and enjoy the view. While the children were sleeping upstairs and I was alone downstairs, I opened the garage door. The morning light was beautiful to see as I was getting ready to serve breakfast. When I looked at the view I felt fear totally take me over. All at once the pine trees and stone drive way of my dreams were directly in front of me. It was the same in every way as my dream. Not one stone was out of place. I knew at that time what I was running away from and where I was running to. I was running out of my home to the neighbors for help. I had a little blonde girl aged three, a blonde boy almost two years old. I had on my designer jeans, and I was pregnant. Could this child to be, be the something I was missing when I was running out of my home? Was I in tears because I could not save the baby? Talk about racing thoughts, I sure had them. I was scared to death to live in that place when I realized that I was looking at the same view that was in my dreams.

Needless to say, I did not have a clue what to do. Why did I have this dream? I knew I had to do something. I knew I had to try to change the outcome of this dream. I wanted to alter the possible tragedy or the destiny of this dream. I had my little girl's hair cut very short. I wanted my son out of diapers. That boy got potty trained real fast and was good at it, too. Some days my son would use a toilet or a garbage can or open a cupboard door. I did not care if he made a mistake, I was just glad he was out of diapers. I had my home changed from propane gas heat to a total electric heat. I believe I was one of the first to buy the Jen Air Electric Glass stovetop. The house was total electric, because I believed nothing would blow up if it was electric. The only thing that could would be the transformer if over loaded. That transformer was far from my home. Yes, electric could start a fire, but this fire in my dream was from a huge explosion. One thing I could not change was that there was a small air strip about five miles on the other side of my woods. Between my home and the air strip was nothing but trees and cows with a pasture just behind my home.

I took control of what I could, but I had no control of the air craft and their flight patterns. It was a small airport, the kind where they gave lessons to fly a small air craft. Anyone could learn to fly a two or four seat plane. This is the one thing that could cause the explosion that I had in my dream. A plane crashing into my home would definitely cause the kind of explosion that was in my dreams. I learned a few years later if I had no control over the planes or the air field, I knew someone that did. His name is Jesus! As a regular daily prayer I would pour the precious blood of Jesus over all of my property. My home was covered by the blood of the Lamb. I was covered by Jesus Christ Mutual Life Insurance. I had a dynamite retirement plan, and the cost was already picked up by the agent. Amen!

Was this dream a forewarning from God or His enemy? I don't like to say his name. I do not want any credit or glory going to the enemy. I am sure you have a name for him. Where do you think this dream came from? Was it from one of God's angels or an angel from the dark side? Was this the Holy Spirit or a nightmare?

This is what I believe about this dream. It was because I moved into the Bible belt of western New York that I learned the Word. I learned the love of Jesus from so many different denominations, all praying for me. It was the place I needed to be. The enemy was trying to do everything to destroy the truth. This enemy did not want me saved. This bad angel wanted me to be in fear, or even move to keep me away from those Christians that were part of my salvation. Yet I know today that he did not have a chance. There is much power in numbers in prayer. I was not filled with the Holy Spirit when I first received this dream. Yet, I sure was full of the Holy Spirit when I poured the blood of Jesus over my home. I did have my insurance paid for with the CEO called Jesus Christ, the owner of Jesus Christ Mutual Life Insurance. Many call him God. I had His authority with the power of the Holy Spirit to have the privilege with the job of protecting my children. I was covered. Everything and all that was on my five acres was insured, and covered with His Blood! I was safe to live in my dream home. Nothing would take away what was given to me by God. No power in heaven, on earth or in the universe is stronger than the Love of God that He has for me and for you.

Does it matter? If from God, He arrived in time. If

from the enemy, he failed. In the word of God an angel will come to you in a dream. God Is Good!

Matthew 1:20 ... *As he considered this, an angel of the Lord appeared to him in a dream. "Joseph, son of David," the angel said, "do not be afraid to take Mary as your wife. For the child within her was conceived by the Holy Spirit.*

John2:28 ... *"Then, after doing all those things, I will pour out my Spirit upon all people. Your sons and daughters will prophesy. Your old men will dream dreams, and your young men will see visions.*

"What Say You"

Notes and comments!

Chapter 2

The Tractor with a Piggy Back Hay Wagon!

This occurred after my death experience. After the accident with one night in Warsaw Hospital, I was advised to see my own OGBYN. The hour and half drive home in a VW Bug was a rocky ride. When I arrived home I was bleeding. Off to my OGBYN doctor and then into Mercy Hospital. I was then hospitalized again this time in Mercy Hospital on Abbot Road in the City of Buffalo. I had to stay in bed 24/7. Complete bed rest to save my baby. Every day I was losing too much blood from the placenta.

I had a priest visit me for a *pre birth blessing*. I asked to please *baptize* this baby that is still in my womb (*A special mother's blessing*).

One night I started going into labor. I called the nurse station to inform them. The nurse said the doctor just left you not long ago. The doctor gave me something to help me sleep and they were thinking that the medication was talking. Again I called the nurse station and informed them that I just gave birth to a baby boy. "Are you sure?" they asked me.

I was getting a little angry with them not believing me. I said in an angry voice, "I have a little son between my legs and I would like someone to help him. He is a tiny little thing. Also I would like someone to clean me and the bed. Hurry, my son needs help!" Soon a teenage volunteer candy striper came into the room. She then called the nurse station and said, "There really is a baby and I need someone to help me." I said, "The 'Help Me Line' was getting longer." Two nurses came running into my room. They put my baby boy on a paper table matt. The candy striper carried him out of my room with hands holding him as far from her as possible. By the look on her face you would think she was holding a deadly virus. She carried him down to the preemie section of the hospital were those nurses cleaned him up. I will never get that picture out of my mind. Instead of wrapping him in a blanket or holding him close to her heart, he was carried out with nothing on him and at arm's length. I just knew that he was not going to spend much time with us on earth. I took some water from my bed side and I baptized my son David Paul before anyone came into the room. He lived for only two hours and I was discharged the next day. I called my husband so he would be able to see his son before David Paul passed away. He made it in time and I was glad for that.

With so many weeks in bed, I needed to get out of the house and go for a ride in the car. A nice ride along Lake Eire taking in the fresh air would help me feel a little better. Some would say I had cabin fever and needed to get out and see some sites. My husband took me for a half hour drive south on route five. After thirty minutes I was ready to turn around and get back home. My husband was driving the VW Bug. It was called a bug because it is a very small vehicle size and shape. We were driving on the right lane of the road. Then out of nowhere, a tractor was crossing the two lanes with two full hay wagons, one hooked up to the other. The tractor was pulling piggy back, so they call it. I screamed to my husband to stop and he kept driving as if he did not see it. I screamed again and I grabbed the wheel to pull the car off the road. Richard, my husband, yelled back to me "what the hell are you doing." He pulled the wheel back and I covered my head and was ready for impact. Then I looked up, turned my head around to see what happened to the hay wagons. I looked out the back window of the VW and there was no tractor or wagons. I saw it clear as day. Yet there was nothing to be seen. Again my husband asked me what my problem was. I said, "Did you see the tractor and the two hay wagons?" "No, what are you talking about?" I thought the car was so small that we went under it. But we did not. Only I saw it. It really wasn't there. I told that story many times.

One night when I was returning home from my sister-in-law's home in Buffalo, I told that story. That story was fresh in my mind returning home. That night we girls were talking about strange stories and I just finished telling that story about the tractor and the hay wagons. After about one hour drive on RT 78, one mile from my driveway, I saw the same tractor pulling the same two hay wagons. My heart started to race and I knew I had to move. When the tractor was approaching the turn, it started to get closer to me. I took advantage of the driveway of the Wyoming Rod & Gun Club. I drove into the drive way and made sure I was not near the road as the tractor approached the turn. And sure as I am typing this on my lap top, the wagons fish-tailed and took up both lanes. If I had not had that vision, I would have been in an accident for sure. Soon the farmer retrieved control again of both wagons. Soon the tractor and wagons were back in their own lane. I was saved from another accident. I left the safety of the Gun Club driveway, my vehicle and I returning home intact. Was this vision from an Angel or a Demon?

"What Say You?"

Myself, I believe both were at work at the same time. One power was out to destroy me and the other power to protect me. I remember the nuns saying that on one shoulder is an angel always whispering in your ear. On the other shoulder is the devil shouting into the other ear. When you are walking with the Lord, Trust me, silence is loud. I do believe that at the time I saw the vision, this was a vision that came from the Lord for the future.

Notes and comments!

Chapter 3

The Blizzard of 1977

When this blizzard hit Western New York, anyone that was old enough to remember knew just where they were and what they were doing. It was like one of those times you never forget. When JFK and Dr. King was killed or that terrible day of September 11, you knew just where you were, what you were doing and the feeling you felt when that transpired. It is the same as the blizzard of 77.

When this blizzard hit, I was home with three young children. My husband was snowed in at the steel plant. Blankets and food were dropped into the plant for those that had to keep working. My husband was working in the coke ovens, nine battery; these ovens had to be protected to keep up the heat. To have them run save, it takes weeks to heat the special bricks up and weeks to cool them down. This blizzard made it crucial to have the men keep working. My husband had food, clothing and shelter. Sleep on the other hand was a gift when you were able to take a nap. He worked three eight hour shift and rested and then back to start another shift. The paycheck was great, but he sure did earn it.

Carol Quintana

Myself, I was home in Java Center, New York. I had to look after the three children. I had to make sure the food supply did not run out. No one had any idea when the snow would let up and the roads would open again.

We had a freezer full of meat and home grown vegetables. It was the milk, bread, eggs and the everyday food you need that I had to think about. Did we have laundry soap, dish and body soap and shampoo to keep us all clean? Was there toilet paper to last? We were living in a total electric home. I had to think about what to feed the children if we lost power. We had a wood burning stove for heat and maybe fry something on the top of the cast iron wood burning stove. That would have been a big maybe? It took a very long time to boil water on the top of this stove, so I knew this would not be a good item to cook on if we lost power. I knew we were low on dog food, so this I had to ration.

I was not sure if the water to the barn would freeze. I was in total control for looking after the children, our dogs and the live stock in the barn. The barn and the animals in the barn were never my responsibility. The boys always helped their dad in the barn. We had a water pump that would push the water back down four feet into the ground when we shut the water off. I told the boys to feed all the animals the best they knew. Trust me, just trying to get to the barn took my two boys about thirty minutes to accomplish. It is normally only a two minute walk. It was exhausting to walk in snow that was taller than you. My guess is that snow drifts were about twelve feet or more. The drifts were as high as the roof of our home. I had to watch the boys to make sure they did not fall deep into the snow. I gave them directions to pack the snow before walking on it. The boys, all bundled up, were jumping on the snow to pack it. It was such fun for them, but a big worry for me. I did not take my eyes off them till they waved to me from the barn. They could not wait to make snow tunnels and play. They did not have a clue about the seriousness of this blizzard. My advice to the boys was to keep the one barn door open for any or all the animals to go out to eat snow if the water would freeze. We had horses, cows, sheep and pigs with barn cats. The animals had to fend for them self's to keep warm with each other and deal with the food the boys would give them. I would pray they had water and snow to eat. So the responsibility to care for the animals was up to seven and eight year old boys.

My daughter was in charge of the fire wood and keeping the fire going. When the boys returned from the barn, it was then time for me to explain the situation. With a very firm voice and a closed fist, I made it clear if anyone opened the refrigerator, freezer or went to eat anything without my permission, they would get a licking that they would never forget.

I had a leather strap hanging on the side of the steps going to their bedrooms that they all had the pleasure to feel across their butt one time or another. They knew I meant business. It was not a time to refuse to comply with their mother. My daughter knew the situation about the dog food. She was concerned about the small amount of food that I allowed for the dog. There was a huge block of cheese in the refrigerator. She decided to sneak into the refrigerator and cut a piece of cheese for our house dog "Missy." As I walked into the kitchen she was hiding behind the cupboard with a steak knife in one hand and a slice of cheese in the other.

When I saw her I had the look of a mad woman ready to kill. She was terrified as I went to grab the cheese. She put her two hands up to protect herself. It was then the steak knife went in and all the way up the side of her nose. Bridgette was very lucky because the knife went in very close to her eye. I reacted by pulling her two arms down. As I did that, I caused a sawing reaction with the knife coming out of her nose. I grabbed the first rag that was close to me and put it over her nose. It was a nasty dirty dish rag, but I just reacted and grabbed the rag to stop the blood till I got her head over the sink. I rinsed her face, and then washed out the cut with alcohol. I put on a clean cloth and had my daughter apply pressure.

There was no way to get any medical help. I could not take her to a doctor or hospital. I could not even get out of the drive way. We were stuck at home with no one to help, other than the Lord. So I went to the Lord in prayer. I called the boys and we all laid on our hands on Bridgette. We all prayed for a healing. I prayed for a miracle healing. After we prayed, I looked at the cut again. It was no longer bleeding. It had a zig zag cut as if I was sawing the flesh off her nose. There was only a millimeter of flesh that was not cut, keeping the flesh on her nose. All of this took place in about five minutes. My first reasonable thinking was to clean and call the boys and pray. And that is just what we did.

The following thing for me to do was to call my girlfriend Millie. I and my children would cross-country ski with her.

Her husband was a member on the emergency volunteer fire department in North Java. I called Millie and asked her what to do next. She was also a Christian and went to prayer meetings with me at Saint Catherine's in West Seneca. She has seen the power of healing many times and knew the power of prayer. So we said another prayer together. Next, Millie and her husband put on their snowshoes and walked to my home through the woods and pastures. They walked in snowshoes about six miles in the cold and snow. It took at least one hour before they arrived at my door. Millie's husband took off the cloth that my daughter was holding on her nose and was very much surprised. He said to me "When did this happen?" I replied, "Moments before I called." "Not possible, this is already healed." The open cut was closed," it is best that I do nothing. I do not want to open it up to clean it, because it has been taken care of, nothing needs to be done." I don't think he believed me, yet he did. Millie smiled and looked at me as if this was a great testament for her husband about the power in prayer, laying on of hands for healing. As soon as they warmed up, they were on their way back home out in the blizzard with snow shoes on. They wanted to be home, in case another emergency call came in. After a very short time, the only evidence that this accident happened was one freckle on her nose did not match up.

Myself, I have no doubt in my mind. This is a gift from God. Healing comes from the power of the Holy Spirit. This is one of the gifts of the Holy Spirit, and at the time I was part of the healing ministry at church. I have put my hands on many people with Father Leonard and the Holy Spirit healed. I have seen many miracles in the healing ministry. This time

Carol Quintana

I was on my own and had to practice what I preached. God Is Good!

Spiritual Gifts ... **1 Corinthians 12:1-31** ... *Now about spiritual gifts, brothers, I do not want you to be ignorant. 2 You know that when you were pagans, somehow or other you were influenced and led astray to mute idols. 3 Therefore I tell you that no one who is speaking by the Spirit of God says, "Jesus be cursed," and no one can say, "Jesus is Lord," except by the Holy Spirit. 4 There are different kinds of gifts, but the same Spirit. 5 There are different kinds of service, but the same* Lord. *6 There are different kinds of working, but the same God works all of them in all men. 7 Now to each one the manifestation of the Spirit is given for the common good. 8 To one there is given through the Spirit the message of wisdom, to another the message of knowledge by means of the same Spirit, 9 to another faith by the same Spirit, to another gifts of healing by that one Spirit, 10 to another miraculous powers, to another prophecy, to another distinguishing between spirits, to another speaking in different kinds of tongues, and to still another the interpretation of tongues. 11 All these are the work of one and the same Spirit, and he gives them to each one, just as he determines. 12 The body is a unit, though it is made up of many parts; and though all its parts are many, they form one body. So it is with Christ. 13 For we were all baptized by one Spirit into one body—whether Jews or Greeks, slave or free—and we were all given the one Spirit to drink. 14 Now the body is not made up of one part but of many. 15 If the foot should say, "Because I am not a hand, I do not belong to the body," it would not for that reason cease to be part of the body. 16 And if the ear should say, "Because I am not an eye, I do not belong to the body," it would not for that reason cease to be part of the body. 17 If the whole body were an* *eye, where would the sense of hearing be? If the whole body were an ear, where would the sense of smell be? 18 But in fact God has arranged the parts in the body, every one of them, just as he wanted them to be. 19 If they were all one part, where would the body be? 20 As it is, there are many parts, but one body. 21 The eye cannot say to the hand, "I don't need you!" And the head cannot say to the feet, "I don't need you!" 22 On the contrary, those parts of the body that seem to be weaker are indispensable, 23 and the parts that we think are less honorable we treat with special honor. And the parts that are unpresentable are treated with special modesty, 24 while our presentable parts need no special treatment. But God has combined the members of the body and has given greater honor to the parts that lacked it, 25 so that there should be no division in the body, but that its parts should have equal concern for each other. 26 If one part suffers, every part suffers with it; if one part is honored, every part rejoices with it. 27 Now you are the body of Christ, and each one of you is a part of it. 28 And in the church God has appointed first of all apostles, second prophets, third teachers, then workers of miracles, also those having gifts of healing, those able to help others, those with gifts of administration, and those speaking in different kinds of tongues. 29 Are all apostles? Are all prophets? Are all teachers? Do all work miracles? 30 Do all have gifts of tongues. 29 Are all apostles? Are all prophets? Are all teachers? Do all work miracles? 30 Do all have gifts of healing? Do all speak in tongues? Do all interpret? 31 But eagerly desire the greater gifts.*

1 Corinthians 12:11 ... *But one and the same Spirit works all these things, distributing to each one individually just as He wills.*

Romans 12:6 ... *Since we have gifts that differ according* to the grace given to us, each of us is to exercise them accordingly: if prophecy, according to the proportion of his faith;

Ephesians 4:11... *And He gave some as apostles, and some as prophets, and some as evangelists, and some as pastors and teachers,*

Hebrews 2:4 ... *God also testifying with them, both by signs and wonders and by various miracles and by gifts of the Holy Spirit according to His own will.*

John 4:48 ... *So Jesus said to him, "Unless you people see signs and wonders, you simply will not believe."*

"What Say You?"

Notes and comments!

Chapter 4

Let The Blind See!

One of my friends, who attended the prayer meetings with mass, personal testimonies, altar calls and the laying on of hands for the healing ministry, was in need of prayer for her daughter. For no apparent reason, her daughter lost her sight. One day she was fine and the next day she was blind. She took her daughter to doctors for tests and they could not find out the answer for the girls blindness. I suggested that she take her daughter to the prayer meeting. "Give it over to God" I said.

For months there was no help to be had with the doctors. Finally, after much endurance on the doctor's road she was disgusted and totally drained. She was so tired running from one doctor to another; she decided to ask God for help.

The night came to turn over this situation to the Lord. My friend did see many miracles in the healing ministry and she was afraid of disappointment. She witnessed events that appeared to be contrary to the laws of nature. All that she witnessed were regarded as an act of God. The prayer meeting would end and was followed by prayer for the healing of her beautiful daughter. The time came when father prayed with his hands on her head and the elder's hands on the shoulders, called on the blood of Jesus to cover, protect and heal the blindness. Father called on the power of the Holy Spirit; in the name of Jesus who with the same prayer cast out any ungodly demons. All together, everyone in the room had their hands lifted high in prayer. Her daughter was slain in the spirit and her eyes opened and a clear vapor started leaving her eyes. At once she started to see light. In a few days she had a total healing. I guess you can say, she found a new doctor. His name is Jesus. I say to myself, this is an easy one, the healing power of the Holy Spirit. This is a gift from God.

"What Say You?"

Notes and comments!

Chapter 5

The Most Unforgivable Horseback Ride!

At this time all of my children were old enough to go horseback riding. We had many horses and we were in the buying and selling business of them. When I found one I really liked, this one we would keep. I wanted to make sure we all had a safe and dependable horse to ride. After a few years, I found the perfect horse for me. Her name was Afro. Her breed was a Morgan. She had beautiful long mane and tail. Her head looked like a chess piece. She was a barrel and game horse ready to perform as soon as you were in the saddle. She was the gentlest horse of all, but by the way she performed you would think I was riding a mad beast. She loved to run. I did not have a suitable horse for the boys at this time.

I did have a horse named Dandy Babe that was over sixteen hands tall. He was a lot of horse and large enough to carry all three of my children. He was a proud cut gelding and was half quarter horse and half thoroughbred. His color was a black and white paint. This horse hated me, but he loved my daughter. He was only gentle for her. My daughter Bridgette was in the saddle and had the reins in her hands. Her brother

Richard was also in the saddle holding on to her, and the youngest, Steven, was on the back of the horse holding on to Richard. With three on one horse, this would be a stroll down RT 78.

Bridgette was very good with Dandy Babe and never had any problem with him. After our slow ride, I wanted to open up and run with my horse. This is something I could not do in this situation. I asked Bridgette to take Dandy Babe into the barn and I would follow in a few minutes. I wanted my children off the horse and the horse in the barn before I opened up my Afro to run like lightning back to the barn. I did not know that Dandy Babe stopped half way up the drive way to the barn. Dandy Babe was looking for Afro and would not listen to Bridgette as hard as she tried. My driveway had a shape like the letter S and I could not see around the turn that Dandy Babe was still in the drive way. I assumed they were all safe in the barn.

It was my time in the saddle to do my thing on the back of Afro. Again, I assumed all things were in place for a safe run. I was to start my run up the six hundred foot double figure S drive way and then another thousand feet to the barn. He- Haw with a kick and off we went. Afro went flying up the driveway. When we turned the first corner of the S in the driveway I knew I had a serious problem. At the speed I was traveling, all I had time for was a cry to Jesus for help. Dandy Babe was ready for a race and off like a flash as soon as we turned the corner. Bridgette and Richard were holding on tight. Steven, on the other hand, could not hold on. Both of his little hands opened up as if he was about to be nailed to the cross. Steven was falling in slow motion between the horse's hind legs. He was soon just inches away from hitting the ground. Dandy Babe was ready to crush him with his huge hooves and most likely kill him. My baby boy was about to be killed in front of my eyes. There was nothing that I could do. I cried out in horror to Jesus for help. Next, I saw a set of enormous spiritual hands lift up Steven and set him back in his place on Dandy Babe's back. Like a flash of lightning, Steven wrapped his two little arms around his brother Richard.

I saw the hands; they were holding my son. They moved his little body from face down to the ground to his starting position on the back of Dandy Babe. Steven had the look of amazement and did not know what just happened, but whatever it was, he was glad about it. And believe it or not, it did not surprise me. I was relieved, happy with tears of joy, but not surprised. These enormous spiritual hands were very familiar. I knew that I had seen them before. The spiritual experiences in my life and the life of my children started to become the norm. God Is Good!

"What Say You?"

Acts 10:3 ... *About the ninth hour of the day he clearly saw in a vision an angel of God who had just come in and said to him, "Cornelius!"*

Notes and comments!

Chapter 6

The Light Bulb!

This is a short but sweet little story. Does this sound unbelievable, yes? Is it true, yes? This experience is the one that my son Richard remembers the most, as far as not being possible. We live in the beginning of our new total electric home. We did have a wood burning stove that we used every day in the winter time for heat. With the doors closed on the fireplace, you did not receive any light, but we always had heat. This one night we heard a loud popping noise and then an explosive sound. This noise was related to the shutting down of all our electric power. I went to investigate the situation and I saw that the blinking red light that should be on the transformer was not on. No blinking red light; we had a dead transformer. As it turned out, the transformer that supplied our home with electricity had blown out. I called the electric company and they said they would send someone out. We were not the only home that was affected by this blowout. There were many homes that depended on that one transformer.

I never knew what caused the problem, but it took many

Journey into the Light

hours before it was fixed. With no power it was a good night to go to bed early. It took a little time in the darkness to find the rope that was connected to our pull down stairs. It was those stairs that we used to get upstairs to our one huge bedroom. I had my three children go up first. Then I took a bucket and toilet paper upstairs with me, just in case one or more had to go to the bathroom. Once we were all upstairs I used an old bed spring to cover the hole created by the pull down stairs. In the dark, it would be very easy to fall down those stairs. Once all my children were in bed, I said "let all of us hold hands and pray together." We all joined hands and I led a prayer. I asked that the transformer would be repaired or replaced safely, protecting those that had to go out in this cold night to do that job. I asked that all our neighbors be warm and safe. I then asked God for light as soon as possible. The next thing that happened was the one light bulb upstairs came on. It was the only light bulb that went on. We had no power of any kind on any item in our home, but we had one light bulb providing us with light.

Richard jumped up and walked over to the light switch. Richard turned the switch to the off and on position and nothing changed. The light stayed on. That was truly a miracle. I believe that God goes a little more out of His way when children pray. We all need to be like little children to our God the Father! After that night, I always asked my children to pray with me when prayer was needed. I was part of a prayer chain and when I received a call to pray for whatever, my children were included in the prayers.

What would you say about this experience? Myself, I give the glory to God. I believe an angel occupied that light bulb and we were looking at a little of the light that comes from heaven. Was this from Angel's or Demons? Was this Spiritual or Supernatural?

Acts 12:7 ... *And behold, an angel of the Lord suddenly appeared and a light shone in the cell; and he struck Peter's side and woke him up, saying, "Get up quickly." And his chains fell off his hands.*

Acts 5:19 ... *But at night an angel from the Lord opened the doors to their cell and led them out of the prison.*

Matthew 28:2 ... *And behold, a severe earthquake had occurred, for an angel of the Lord descended from heaven and came and rolled away the stone and sat upon it.*

Acts 8:26... *But an angel of the Lord spoke to Philip saying, "Get up and go south to the road that descends from Jerusalem to Gaza." (This is a desert road.)*

Acts 27:23 ... *"For this very night an angel of the God to whom I belong and whom I serve stood before me,*

When it comes down to it, if it be light, work or a message that God wants done, he calls an angel to get it done.

"What say you?"

Notes and comments!

Chapter 7

The Charismatic Conferences of the World!

At this time in my life, I am very involved in the Charismatic movement in the Catholic Church. I was in the healing ministry and teaching in my parish. And one of the things I enjoyed the most was every week I would introduce someone from my parish or the neighboring parishes to my Tuesday night prayer meeting. They would experience for the first time the power of the Holy Spirit and hear the testimonies and see the miracles of The Holy Spirit first hand. After one visit to the prayer meeting, whoever I took wanted to buy a Bible and start reading the word. I was one of many members of this Church elected to go to the conferences to represent Western New York. I was to come back to the prayer meetings and share all that I could with my parish, Saint Patrick's. I would share my stories to members of the Bible study. I remember buying a book that was going to be published about the conference that we received many weeks later. I remember my friend, Millie, borrowed my book to read. To her amazement, everything she read, she already heard from me. This is proof, when you feed the Holy Spirit with his word, that whenever it is needed, you will be able to share it. And for the seven day conference the Holy Spirit poured over the stadium in Kansas City that held over sixty thousand and we were just filled with knowledge.

When I knew that I was going to the conference, I asked a good friend Rita if she wanted to drive with me. We became friends when I started working as a waitress at the Sattler Hotel Jewish Deli. We both, at that time had sons the same age, twelve. We took her son Lee and I took my son Richard.

We decided to make it a long drawn out road trip. Maybe we would drive only four hours a day. From Buffalo, NY the first stop would be Cleveland, Ohio. We wanted to enjoy the pools and the night life that the motels had to offer. We planned to have a holy experience and a vacation at the same time. This was to be Rita's first prayer meeting ever, with sixty thousands hands lifted in prayer and everything else that would be scheduled for the seven days. She did not have a clue what to expect.

The morning that we left, Rita noticed a cloud in the sky that was the shape of a cross. I said, "No, that must be from some kind of aircraft" The cross in the sky was so thin; I never saw a cloud that thin. Would you believe it? Four hours later that cross was still in the sky. This was just the beginning of our spiritual events. The first night we stayed in a beautiful motel with a beautiful pool. We stayed up late and we slept late, much more than we should have. We drove to eat our breakfast at Denny's and to our surprise the cross was still in the sky.

We planned our next stop around which town had the

Journey into the Light

best motel with a great pool. Our plans were to have a pool at each overnight stop. It was in the summer time and the temperatures were in the high eighty's. I was driving an old Ford station wagon with wood grain side panels that I had purchased just weeks before we left. I could not get the air conditioner to work, and we were roasting at every stop sign or red light. At the next overnight stop, we had a better pool than the night before and they had live music at the bar. Funny but true, we started talking to a few young men to see if they could get our air condition working. We were having a little harmless flirting for a good cause. One man said he would look at my car and see what he could do. He opens the hood and said, "Lady, whose car is this?" I said, "It is my car" Then he said, "I don't know what you two ladies are up too, but this car does not have air conditioning!" I must say, I did feel like a fool. Since the car had all these vents on the dash board, I just assumed it had air.

The next day was so hot that I pulled over to the side of the road where sprinklers were on. I stopped the car and stood over the sprinklers. I did that more than once. I looked as if I was in a wet T-Shirt contest. But I did cool down and my shirt was dry in a few minutes with those temperatures.

The next evening we had it all planned on which exit to get off, to stay at this absolutely beautiful motel. I said to Rita, "We have only one more exit to go and we can dive into the pool!" I no longer finished that statement; my hands froze to the steering wheel. Something was pulling the wheel off the exit that I was at. Rita said, "What are you doing?" I answered, "I don't have a clue?" "I don't know why I did that. I had no control in the matter, it just happened" The next thing was a photo of a gorgeous motel and pool at the end of the ramp. It had this sign on the road with an arrow pointing and the words reading just one mile on the right. I looked at Rita and she looked at me and we said, "Why not, it looks good." So we drove the one mile and registered at that motel rather than the one we planned on stopping at.

We got the boys ready for bed and we put on the TV. We soon realized that we just drove over a time line. The news was on. The boys were rough-housing around the room and Rita and I listened to the news. To our surprise, we realized we were four very lucky people. The motel that we planned to stay at was just robbed. They first robbed the office and shot and killed the employees. They knocked on each door and robbed everyone who was staying at that motel. Some were beaten, others shot. Some ran. It was a terrible thing for all those people and their families and friends. The first thing I did was call my son Richard to pray with me. We held hands and I first started to pray for those men that did this horrible thing. Rita was so surprised that I was praying for them, the men that did this terrible thing. They need our prayers the most; we don't want them to do this again. They need to find the Truth and stop this life style. Can you think about the testimony they would be able to give if they find the Lord and change their lives. How many lives can they bring to the Lord if they are saved? Next, still holding each other's hands, I lifted up all those souls who were killed in this terrible robbery and for their family and friends to receive the peace beyond human reason, may all their needs be met. All night I could not sleep. I had racing thoughts all night. Why was my car taken off the road leading us to a safe motel? Yes, I believed in God! I am sure most or all of the other people in that motel did too. Am I so special? I don't think so. Where was my answer to this question? I was troubled by this. Why were we saved or spared from this terrible robbery?

When I arrived at the conference, I shared this with some of my friends, elders and friends from different denominations. Then I saw Father Leonard and I grabbed the opportunity to speak to him on this matter. After I shared my story, I wanted to find the answer to the question, why was I spared from this robbery and maybe even death? Father explained that we are like a fine tuned shortwave radio. The closer we walk with Jesus, the less static there is on the shortwave radio. The further away the walk, the more static there is on the radio and it is hard to hear what is being said. God was speaking to every one of those people. You were just one that heard His voice. There were three or four empty rooms at that motel that night. This makes me believe three or four more groups heard His voice too. I believe many more lives were saved that night. I must say that I was satisfied with that explanation. I am not that special; I am a child of God like everyone else. Can you just imagine this world if everyone could hear God clear as a bell? This would be one beautiful planet to live on.

"What Say You?"

I say Father Leonard was correct. The Holy Spirit does speak to all of us. Are we all listening?

Notes and comments!

Chapter 8

My Daughter's Accident, Face down in the Fire!

My first born was a girl, Bridgette. In her teens she developed a seizure disorder. One morning she was stoking the hot coals in an old homemade wood stove. She was twenty six with a six year old son, living in the country with her father at this time. She went downstairs to stoke the coals. She put more wood in the stove, to warm the cold morning, not knowing that her son was following. She was on her knees stoking the hot coals. Then out of the blue, she had a seizure and fell face down in the coals. Thank God her son was with her. He was six years old and he took his mother by the hand and kept pulling and guiding her up the stairs. She was like a walking zombie when she was in a seizure mode. Her dad and I were divorced at that time. I was living in the City of Buffalo. I received a call that my daughter was in an accident and was burned. She had burned her entire face in the coals and her neck on the cast iron stove. Her father called the Short Tract Volunteers Fire Department. Karl took the call that night. Karl Kipple drove her to Wellsville Jones Memorial Hospital. All they could do is stabilize her. Then Jones Memorial made the decision to have her transported to ECMC burn treatment center.

Carol Quintana

This accident is a book all by itself. Someday I pray that my daughter tells this story in a book for all to read. I just want to share one incident at ECMC hospital.

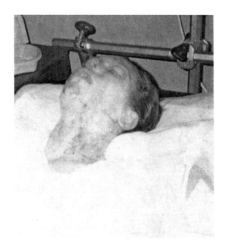

Dec. 7, 1992

My daughter Bridgette first and second day in ECMC Burn Treatment.

Through it all God was at her side every moment.

I pray that God would send a good plastic surgeon.

Journey into the Light

But it is what it is and she loves the Lord. After 17 surgeries she has a smile on her face. She still needs surgery about every five years.

Mother's tears never end but the Lord wipes them away every day. One day at a time sweet Jesus, one day at a time.

I believe it was my third or fourth visit when I was waiting to see my daughter. There was much to do before you would visit anyone with burns. The doctor was checking her eyes to see if she lost any of her vision. I thank God that she did not. As I sat in this room, where only severely ill or serious accident patients were, I listened to the crying of a mother and family members. Her son was in a very bad snow mobile accident. The son, while driving, lost control for whatever reason. He was almost dead when he arrived. It was very serious and there was little chance for this young man to make it. The accident was close to Rushford Lake and I believe the family had a snowmobile business. The boy was very skilled in driving and knew the dos and don'ts about safe driving. This accident should not have happened. But for some reason it did. At high speed, in the snow, it is very easy to miss a wire, branch or a fence. My heart was breaking for the mother and family. I walked up to her and asked her, "Would you mind if we all hold hands and say a prayer for your son?" Just like that everyone started to hold hands and I joined in and lead them all in a prayer. I asked her the name of her son and I said the name and lifted him up to Jesus. I asked for a miracle healing and to give the doctors the skill and knowledge to work on this boy so that he would be made whole. I prayed with the power of the Holy Spirit and the blood of Jesus.

I did not know their denomination, but they were of the Christian faith. I prayed for some time and gave a hug and a kiss to all. Then the doctors called me into the clean room to get me ready to see my daughter and inform me about her eye sight. I received a thank you and off I went, never to see or hear from that family again. We were like two ships passing in the night. Many weeks later, I went to a prayer group in Java Lake and a girl told a story about her friend's family. It seems that her friend's son was in a snow mobile accident and was sure to die. Out of the blue an angel walked up to the mother and asked to hold hands and pray. Many hours later, the doctors came out of surgery and said they were very lucky. They were able to do everything needed to save him. He was still recovering, but he will be like new. She said that the surgery scar will not even be seen when it all heals. I never felt so blessed. This mother called me an angel. I wish I was able to remain silent, but it is not my nature.

I said to my friend Linda, "I was never called an angel before. That was me in the room praying with that mother and family." All the ladies in the room started talking at the same time. It was like watching "The View" on TV. That is when I learned that they had the snowmobile business and how the accident took place out by Rushford Lake. I never asked those unnecessary questions at the time of prayer. I just asked for his first name that I don't even remember today. I will never forget the prayer and the outcome. If the mother or the son by some chance read this, give me a call. Today I live only a few miles from Rushford Lake. I pray that all is still good. This was truly one of the gifts of the Holy Spirit!

The Angels of the Lord took hold of the doctor's hands in

the surgery room, another whispered in the doctors' ear with directions for the proper procedure. The doctors did the most faultless performance ever on a surgical table. No audience to cheer or clap with a standing ovation when the surgery was finished. But you better believe there was a choir of Angels singing in prayer, praising the Father. God Is Good!

"What Say You?"

Notes and comments!

Chapter 9

The Cemetery Stones!

I was a very young child when I either had a dream or really experienced it. I was not sure if it was a dream. My father's home was next to a cemetery that was there from before the war of 1812. This was a very old and simple family cemetery. I grew up with this and never had any problem with a cemetery for a backyard to play in. Side by side was a set of tomb stones that I sat on. One read *Mother,* the other read *Father.* Next to that was a large flat stone about four by eight feet with just a hand on it with a robe like the hand of a monk. I would nap on that stone as if I had a special friend under this stone that looked over me. Then there was a very different stone from all the rest. It was like a huge centerpiece on a table. I always was in awe of the huge stone in the center of the once beautiful family cemetery. It stood over twelve feet tall and it was put together in four parts. One night I looked out my bedroom window, viewing the cemetery and I saw a huge figure of a man dressed like the grim reaper. He raised his head and looked at me in the window, no face to be seen, just a black hole in the hood where a face should be. I was filled with fear for the first and only time with my play yard, the cemetery. Then I saw him, with one blow of his arm, hit the huge stone and it fell into four pieces. Did I see this or was I dreaming? The next morning, I jumped out of bed to look out the window and the stone was in four pieces. I remembered the fear I felt and I did not like anyone or anything messing with my playground. I was afraid and pissed off at the same time. I do not believe this was an angel of God. And I don't believe God would put such fear into a child's heart. Nothing more ever came out of that dream. Why or for what reason, I have not a clue. Then again, not everything is a special message from an angel. It could have been; it was what it was. But it did happen.

"What Say You"

Notes and comments!

Chapter 10

I'm Just A Little Tea Pot!

The first time I ever put my hands on anyone to pray for a healing was a very humbling experience. After many months or maybe a year attending the prayer meetings, an elder approached me and said, "Don't you know that you should be up here with the rest of us when we pray." I was honored to be asked. I felt that I should always be up there with Father and the rest of the healing ministry. But I was thinking that it was my own feelings and not sure that they came from God.

The following week before prayer meeting I fasted and prayed. When I was at prayer meeting, I was just holier than thou. I just could not wait till I put my hand on someone to pray and see the healing take place. And I was going to be the one with hands on. I said to myself, "Holy am I, Carol is going to do the healing." Then when we started to pray for the first person, Father Leonard put his hands on her head and I put my left hand on her shoulder and the right hand lifted up to the heavens. She was asking for prayer to control her sugar. She needed a healing of some kind to keep the sugar in control or just let it be healed. Father did all the praying with the words for all to hear. I was praying in English and then in the Spirit. As soon as I started to pray, a song was going through my head and I could not concentrate on my praying. I had to do everything possible not to smile or laugh. The song was, "I'm a little teapot, short and stout, just tilt me over and pour me out." Over and over this song was singing in my head with the sound of a choir of children singing.

After Father was finished praying for this one lady, I asked if I could speak to him before the next person came forward. I said to Father, "I don't think I am the correct person for the healing ministry." I told him about the song in my head playing over and over and I could not pray. Father said, "What do you think that song means?" I guess Father knew my natural nature better them me. He asked me, "What did you feel when you put your hands on the woman's shoulder and the other hand up to the heavens?" I said, "I felt an enormous warm surge of energy come down my arm that was lifted up and I felt that energy flow into the woman." "There you go," said Father, "do you not know what was being said to you in that song. God knows your nature and He knew you needed to be knocked down a few notches. God was showing you that Carol is nothing more than a teapot." I or any other member in the healing ministry has no power of any kind. We are all servants with these gifts from the Holy Spirit. No one is a healer; all of us in prayer for healing are just a vessel like a teapot. The healing power that goes into the teapot then flows out of the pot and into the person asking for healing. After that discussion, that holier than thou attitude became a humble servant attitude. I must admit that whenever I had a chance to lay my hands on a person to ask for a healing, I jumped on it. But I always made sure that I gave the glory to the Gifts of the Holy Spirit and I was nothing more than a teapot. God Is Good!

"What Say You?"

Notes and comments!

Chapter 11

Do You Need a New Appliance?

This is a short little story. Once I became a member of the healing ministry, I was putting my hand on everyone and everything. My husband was on unemployment at this time and we were living in what was to be our barn. I was breeding German Shepherds and they helped with extra income. In the fifties and sixties the dog to have would be a German shepherd. I guess the TV movie "Rin Tin Tin" helped make them a popular watch dog to have. Today it is the pit bull. I would never want one, but they can be a good dog.

With just one check coming in and no pups for sale to make ends meet, we had to watch every dollar. On this special day my washing machine stopped working. With three children you need a working machine. I don't remember where the children were at the time. I do remember I was alone and I had a ton of laundry to get done. I put my hands on the washing machine that would not spin the water out and prayed that God would fix this machine and keep it working until I had a litter of pups to sell. And yes, after that prayer, the machine started to spin out the water and it stayed in working condition until we had the money to buy another. Was it just good luck? I like to give God the credit. I took out an interest free loan for a machine until we had the cash to buy. I guess you can call it a stimulus check from God.

"What Say You?"

Notes and comments!

Chapter 12

Angels or Demons at the Kitchen Table!

After my near-death experience, I was starting to get into the supernatural. The first thing I was introduced to was an Ouija Board. This is a game that you and friends sit around the table and almost touch the arrow in the center of the board. The letters of the alphabet would be around the board and the words Yes and No. With one or more people setting at the table it will spell out a message for you from the spirit world. I was giving the credit to my great grandmother, that I never knew, when I received a message.

Soon the news of the lady up on the hill playing with the Ouija Board was sent out to every church and prayer group. Thousands of Christians were praying for me. These were people that I never met or knew. I never realized that so many people were praying for me and my family at this time. Due to these people and their prayers, I made a change in my life. To all of you, and you know who you are, "Thank You."

I soon developed a personal relationship with Jesus by reading The Word every day. Once you start reading The

Word, you cannot put the book down. I prayed about the board and the answer was to burn it. Not an easy task. This board is made out of almost indestructible properties. I had to break the board into many pieces with an ax before it would burn. It was late at night and the children were sleeping. I went outside to our burn barrel and put a can of lighter fluid on the pieces of the board and prayed. I asked that all things that are not from God be put at the foot of the cross. I bound them at the foot of the cross with the precious blood of Jesus. I asked God first to protect me and my children and all the live stock in the barn. I remember reading in the Word that there were demons that went into the pigs. I did not want any of that. I covered all of my property and possessions and most of all my children and myself before I cast out those things that were not of God. I kept praying, and for a moment I was not proud of what I said. I said "Burn You Bastard, Burn." Then I went back to praying like a Christian should. Finally, the board started to burn and I heard evil screaming, many voices similar to the voices you would hear in a horror movie. All that was missing was a little girl's head spinning around and vomiting green pea soup. It felt as if I was watching some kind of exorcism. I was not fearful, more like angry. I was angry at myself because I was so full of myself to think I was so special, and to bring such an item into my home. Angry; that I exposed my children to such danger.

> There is a plain and simple answer. There is no hard work to figure this experience out. The Bible is very clear on this matter. I will state just a few words from the Bible. Detestable Practices!

Deuteronomy 18:9-14 ...*When you enter the land the*

LORD your God is giving you, do not learn to imitate the detestable ways of the nations there. 10 Let no one be found among you who sacrifices his son or daughter in the fire, who practices divination or sorcery, interprets omens, engages in witchcraft, 11 or casts spells, or who is a medium or spiritist or who consults the dead. 12 Anyone who does these things is detestable to the LORD, and because of these detestable practices the LORD your God will drive out those nations before you. 13 You must be blameless before the LORD your God.

Deuteronomy 18:10-11 ... *Let no one be found among you who sacrifices his son or daughter in [a] the fire, who practices divination or sorcery, interprets omens, engages in witchcraft, 11 or casts spells, or who is a medium or spiritist or who consults the dead.*

Isaiah 47:13-15 ... *13 All the counsel you have received has only worn you out! Let your astrologers come forward, those stargazers who make predictions month by month, let them save you from what is coming upon you. 14*

Surely they are like stubble; the fire will burn them up. They cannot even save themselves from the power of the flame. Here are no coals to warm anyone; here is no fire to sit by. 15 That is all they can do for you — these you have labored with and trafficked with since childhood. Each of them goes on in his error; there is not one that can save you.

God makes it very clear in his Word. These things do exist, but they are an object of horror and disgust to Him. We have our free will and we can make the correct or incorrect choices. Which power does His children what to have? I want nothing to do in the supernatural world. God gives His Gifts of the Holy Spirit and the devil will counterfeit them all. You need to read the word to learn the difference. One example, having knowledge is not the same as fortune telling. One with the gift of knowledge does not charge you fifty dollars to share that knowledge with you. One that wants to lay on his/her hands to pray for healing does not charge you to do so or depend on it for a paycheck. A love offering is different. Jesus talked about taking nothing and all your needs will be provided for. Jesus and his followers walked town to town and they all had food, clothes and shelter. The Lord will always supply. You should not feel any animosity when a man of God prospers. And you cannot out- give the giver. It is by giving that you receive. All God ever asked for was ten percent, nothing more. If every American just gave one percent to stop the recession, the recession would be over. How much more could ten percent do for God's work? God Is Good!

"What Say You?"

Notes and comments!

CHAPTER 13

The Car Drive Over & Over!

When I and my family first moved into our new barn/kennel we had to soon make some changes. One had to be a four wheel drive vehicle. We had a very steep and long driveway. In the winter time it seemed a little longer. I told all my family and friends, if you don't have a four wheel drive, walk up. I even put a chair to sit on at the half way mark to rest if needed. My friend Alice was coming for a visit one day. She had her mother with her. When she got to my door she was so angry. She said, "Look at you; you are living like the Hollywood Hill Billie's before they made their money. I found it very funny because we were building a little at a time so we would not have a mortgage. Alice and her mother found it very exhausting; it was too strenuous a walk for her mother. I said, "Why did you not sit on the chair and take a rest?" Their replay was, "We did not dare. I was afraid that if I sat in the chair it would start sliding back down the hill and I would have to start the walk all over again." I never forgot that. It was so funny to me, but you had to be there.

The reason I am explaining the drive way is because of the

car that kept driving, in all weather conditions, up the drive. It was not a four wheel drive. It did not have the sound of one. This went on for more than a year. I, my babysitter and my children would hear it. One night my brother heard it and it scared him big time. Many of my friends when they would visit heard it also. It became the talk of the town, among other thing. Remember I was living in the Bible belt of Western New York. Nothing gets by anyone in a small town.

In a small town, things get passed on from town to town. I believe everyone in town knew when I flushed the toilet, and how many sheets of toilet paper I used. That is the nature of small town living. The true reason for everyone knowing everything was to keep an eye on everyone for their needs or look after your home when you were out. Whenever help was needed, it arrived. But the one thing that I wanted to stop arriving is that car. I would hear a car drive up the driveway and stop just feet from my garage door. The engine was never shut off. You would hear someone open the car door and walk around the back of the car. Then in a short time you would hear someone get back into the car and close the door, engine still running. Every time I would go to the door to see who was sitting in the car. Each time I opened the door to look, you would hear silence. Nothing and nobody would be there. And I never heard the car drive down the driveway, just up. This would happen every night, night after night and after a while it just became the norm. It was like living by train tracks and after some time you never would wake up when a train drove by at night. It was a noise that just drifted into the elements of the property. A person that lived in North Java told me that the land I purchased was owned by a young man in love with a young lady and was soon to be married. The driveway was put in by his instructions. They were going to build a log home on these five acres and live happy ever after. The bride died for some reason and he could not deal with the loss of his love. One night he drove up that driveway and got out of the car and did something to the muffler. Then the man got back into the car and he died. I don't know if this was a true story or not. I did not want to follow it through. I just let it be. I said to myself, killing yourself every night must be true hell. To die every night and never to see the one you love again. To me, that sure would be hell.

Can you see killing oneself every night? I don't believe this had anything to do with God. What I do know for sure, when I became Spirit-Filled, I gave my children, property, land, livestock and all my belonging to God. I became His caretaker of all that was given to me. After I gave all that I had to God, the car drive every night came to an end. Was that a true love story that was told to me? I don't have a clue and it does not matter. It does not glorify my Lord so what do I care. Was there something out there every night? I say yes. Did it come from God, I say no. God is good!

"What Say You?"

Notes and comments!

Chapter 14

Her Name Was Susanna!

Before I was spirit filled and still playing with the Ouija Board, I had many supernatural experiences. I had friends that were into astrology, reincarnation, calling on the spirits of the dead. All of them were very interesting but for some reason, I just couldn't get deep into any of it.

One night I was talking on the phone with a friend that was into the spirit world. She was talking to me about the car that was driving up each night and I should help that soul. She was working on my nature as if I was something special. She was doing a good job of it too. She asked me if I could feel anyone present, and I said "Yes." I was able to feel things others could not. I knew when someone was in the room and I would also feel the temperature change. As I was talking to her, a vision of a woman materialized outside my living room window. She looked so much like my sister Diane. She told me that her name was Susanna and she looked as if she was from the late 1800's. She looked just like I did when I was walking up to the heavens with my angel. She spoke to me in the same way my angel spoke to me. I could see myself and see through me also. This is the way Susanna looked and spoke. My friend said to say to her, with authority, "No harm can come to me because I will not allow it" and I believed her. I felt so strong and almighty. One night going up my stairs with Gay visiting for the weekend, she stopped for a moment and said, "Do you see her?" I was amazed that she saw Susanna too. I said, "Yes" Then Gay said, "OK, I am glad you see her too. I am not going crazy." Then off we went to bed as if it was an everyday occurrence.

One of the biggest traps set by Satan is making you believe you have the power and control to do or see the supernatural. You have control and the power to tell the future, the power to talk to the dead, the power to read the stars and so on. It is all just a trap. I thank God every night for all those thousands of people that were praying for me to see the truth. Amen! As stated in the brief little story above. When I gave all of my property over to God, not only did the car stop, Susanna did not return. This spirit that materialized was not from God. They are called evil spirits. They do exist, but not by God instructions. There is up and down and there is good and evil. Like I said earlier, anything good will be counterfeited. There is evil in the world, and when you give your life over for the good and the glory of His name, you are no longer of the world, just in it. Did you ever go and have your fortune told or a Tarot card reading? As Dr. Phil would say on TV, "What were you thinking?" If you need to know what the future holds for you, pick up the Bible and read. It has been the number one best seller for close to two thousand years. It starts with just one chapter a night.

"What say you?"

Notes and comments!

Chapter 15

Phone Prayer!

I was on the phone talking to my sister Elaine. We were not talking about anything special, just passing time. These were the days when I enjoyed the phone. Today, with the computer, I don't enjoy the phone as much. The computer is to the point and you don't have to worry about being the first one to say you want to end the call. But on the other hand, without the voice, you can be misunderstood very easily. This conversation I was having led to her telling me that her son Michael, my Godson, had a very high fever. She told me that she had tried everything, but nothing was working. She was worried, and if it did not go down by the next day, she would take him to the doctor. If it worsened before morning, she would call an ambulance.

Her husband was a fireman and they worked four days at the fire house and four days home. At this time, her husband was at the fire station. The phone did not reach Michael, and they did not have hand phones then to take to his room. I asked my sister when she checked him last. She said "just before I called you." I told her "I pray for the sick all the time and let me tell you, I have seen many healings. Let's pray together, just the two of us for Mike." Elaine agreed, so off I went with my prayers. I think I prayed a little longer due to the fact that no one was putting their hands on him. What did I know? I was new at praying for the sick. When I was finished, I asked my sister to go and check on Mike and give the thank you to Jesus. I received a call in a few minutes informing me that he had no fever. I told my sister, it had nothing to do with me. It was the Holy Spirit and I was just pouring out the prayers like one would pour out a cup of tea. The only difference was that the power was going through the phone lines. No long distance fees, no 800 number, just a strange line that needed no pools to hold up the line. I say a gift of the Holy Spirit!

"What say you?"

Notes and comments!

Chapter 16

Please Bless Our Home!

One day I received a call from a very old friend, Chucky. He was a boy that I liked when I was a kid. He landed up being my sister Diane's brother-in-law. So because of the family ties, we would touch base every so often. He too received the Holy Spirit. His friends needed help in blessing their home. My sister was sharing some of the things that were going on in my life with me and the Church. Because of that conversation with my sister, he decided that I might be a good friend to go with him to bless a home. He was telling me that they called and told him of many strange supernatural things going on in their home. They talked about their firewood that they stacked. It kept falling and sometimes it looked as if it was being pushed. They heated their home for many years with wood and they were not new to stacking firewood. The next strange thing was the items on the fire place mantle would fly across the room. Photos on the walls would turn around. Yes, I would call this strange and supernatural. When I received the phone call from Chucky and he asked me if I would go with him to help with the blessing, I said 'Yes." I felt like "let me at him. I'll cook that goose. Satan, you better start running, Carol is coming." I was so bold, with no fear at all. I would say to people, if I sat up and saw Satan sitting on the side of my bed, I would look at him and say, "Oh, it's only you" and go back to sleep. I am full of the Holy Spirit, covered with the blood of the lamb, what can that looser do to me. That is how it still feels to this day. I am no longer a part of this world, just in it. He can only mislead and harm those that are of the world. The world was given to him to do with as he pleases. Sorry, old man, you can't touch me. If you are a worldly person and need worldly things to be happy, you have a problem. If you have all that the world can offer and you give it all to God, then you are just the caretaker, fear not. That is why when someone truly gives his/her life to Jesus and is baptized by water and the Holy Spirit, it is said "You are no longer of this world, just in it" Below Satan is talking to Jesus.

Luke 4-6 ... *And the devil said to Him, "I will give You all this domain and its glory; for it has been handed over to me, and I give it to whomever I wish.*

This is very clear to me. Who do you serve? Do you want to be of the world or live happily in the world? This is only one explanation why astrology fits so many people. Astrology can fit you like a glove. But when you accept Jesus, you start to read the word. The Word is the food for the Holy Spirit. The more you read the more you grow in the Spirit, the less you are of the world and the less the astrology chart will fit your personality. The enemy has a lot of control over the world. You don't have to be in partnership with it.

I never asked the owners of the house what they were

involved in. The happenings were recent. They were in that home for many years. Something changed and my role was to bring my holy water and pray with Chucky. We went from room to room and I did not feel any ungodly feeling. Just before we started to leave, I asked, "Do you have an attic?" "Yes, we do. Does that matter?" "Absolutely," I said. I did not see an attic, so I had to ask.

At the top of the very steep stairs was a square hole with a board that had to be lifted to enter. It was a full attic but there was no staircase or easy entry to this old attic. To top it off, you needed a ladder or tall stool to slide the light wooden board over the entrance to the attic. Chucky was over six feet and he could not even come close to sliding that board. There was a kitchen stool available. It was that stool that Chucky used to reach the attic. We only needed a small opening to sprinkle a little Holy Water. Just as Chucky started to step on the stool, I felt danger, anger, horror and much more. I cried out "Wait for me." I stood at the top of the stairs and braced myself to hold Chucky. In case he was pushed or fallen, I would break the fall. There was definitely something evil in that attic. It tried to hide, but someone spoke to me and told me to ask about an attic. You cannot run away from God. Every time you try to run away from God, you run into Him. No place to hide. Chucky had no fear and I was ready to back him up. It took all his strength to slide that board. It was no easy task. I kept up with the prayers and had the holy water ready to give to Chucky. He was still fighting with the board when I sprinkled some water on the board and at that moment it moved with ease. We heard noises that I cannot explain. Then Chucky took the Holy Water and sprinkled all four sides of that room. The next occurrence was in a flash the smell of foul air blew through and out the house. It was another good day for the Lord. Chucky got back to me after some time and said all went back to normal after the blessing. That was the first and only time I was called to pray for a healing on a home. It definitely was an experience. I do not know what caused that evil to enter that home. I don't know why it was so dramatic and caused so much activity. If only the TV show <u>Ghost Busters</u> was available, we could have been on a TV show. I am just being silly. I only know that there are angels from God and angels from the dark side. Did you ever have your home blessed? We did and we do. God Is Good!

"What say you?"

Notes and comments!

Chapter 17

Elvis is in the Building!

One of my very best friends, Beverly, called me to see if I wanted to go to the Elvis concert in Buffalo. Absolutely, Yes, Yes, Yes! We were going with her sister-in-law that I never met till that night. We girls were all excited; all wound up and ready to go. Bev and I would go to prayer meetings at Saint Catherin's every Tuesday night, but this night we were going to see Elvis. We were at that time both Spirit-Filled and we would always meet up at Church. Both of us would always bring someone for the first time. This night with Elvis in town and tickets in hand, we drove to pick up her sister-in-law. As Bev and I turned into the cul-de-sac to pick her up, I had a horrifying feeling. I mentioned it to Bev and she said, "Stop that. You scare me when you get those feelings." When we drove into the sister-in-law's driveway, I pointed to a house and said, "It is coming from that home." We were in a hurry and I never did anything else but talked about it to Bev and the sister-in-law. I said, "I should do something," but I did not have an inkling of what to do. So I asked Bev to say a fast prayer with me. The next day, the sister-in-law called Bev and Bev called me. The house that I was pointing to was a friend of the sister-in-law. I believe her name was Rosemary, and Rosemary was very sick and was taken by ambulance to the hospital. She had a blood clot in her brain, was in a coma and it did not look good.

After hearing about Rosemary, I was feeling so guilty. I was thinking that I put Elvis before God. I should have walked over to that house. I should have done something. But what I could have done was a mystery. I talked to Father Leonard about it and he said, "If God wanted you to knock on that door, you would have. I know you, Carol, and you would have done so. If the Holy Spirit was asking you to do it, you would have done so. Introverted, withdrawn or shy you are not. If you were to go in there, you would have gone." Because of this occurrence, Carmel, the sister-in-law went to the next prayer meeting, and she loved it. She asked Rosemary's mother if the prayer group healing ministry led by Father could come and pray over Rosemary. Rosemary's family was Catholic and I did not see a problem with that request. But the mother would not let a priest or any member of this Church come into the hospital room. The mother's words were, "I don't believe in Voodoo Religion." So I said to Carmel, "It is up to you. Rosemary's mother will let you into the room. Rosemary was in a coma for over two weeks and there was no evidence that she would ever wake up. Carmel took the challenge to pray over Rosemary. Carmel went into the room at the designated time. She put her hands on Rosemary and thousands of Christians were praying at the same time. I called every prayer chain I knew. I instructed Carmel on what to do and say before going in. She had a little fear, but she had more love for Rosemary. She was watching the clock and thinking twice about going into the room.

Then as if there was someone behind her, she felt two hands push her into Rosemary's room. So into the room, covered with the Blood of Jesus, she put her hands on Rosemary. First she asked Rosemary to accept Jesus as her personal savior to forgive her of all her sins. Before anything else was said, she felt a response from Rosemary and then continued to pray as instructed. Shortly after that prayer, Rosemary passed away.

When I found out that Rosemary had passed away I felt like a failure. What did not happen that should have? Then with tears in my eyes and heart, I called Father. I received peace after that call. "There are many different kinds of healing" Father said. "Did you ever think that God wanted a spiritual healing? What is more important, healing of the flesh or of the Spirit?" Yes is the answer. I know myself too, and I would have walked into that home bold as brass, if that is what the Lord wanted me to do. We can only do the best that we can with what we have. All I had that night was a horrifying feeling coming out of one house. I gave it my all and I did not give up on Rosemary. Through that experience Carmel found a more personal relationship with the Lord. After a few weeks, all of Bev's friends and family were going to Church together every Tuesday night. This prayer group was growing fast.

Those were very good times and I miss them. Because of so many people attending the prayer group, the fire department had to close the Church down on Tuesday nights. Both sides of the streets for at least half a mile were filled with cars. If there was a need for a fire truck to go by, they could not. So we were broken up into smaller groups with the neighboring Churches. Rosemary was a beautiful young girl. She had never married and had no children. She had her entire life ahead of her. Why she died so young is not for me to question, but I do from time-to-time think about that night. I believe we all wonder why such a young promising life leaves us. The enemy is out there to destroy us. He does not want our flesh but our soul, and God won this one in more than one way. To God I Give The Glory. God Is Good!

"What say you?"

Notes and comments!

Chapter 18

In God We Trust

I heard that the government is going to mint a gold plated dollar piece and it will not have on it "In God We Trust?" This is so sad for the United States of America. Our country was founded on Judean Christian Values and we delete "In God We Trust" on our money. So many wonder why there is a decline in our financial system in this country. We have separated God and Country over and above the normal balance. The town square cannot have a nativity set or anything to remind us of the birth of Christ. Yet no one has a problem with Halloween. This country has lost the importance of life. Both mother and father work just to have more things and let schools and others raise the children. Family values are being lost more every year. It is almost impossible to keep a good marriage going. What is the problem with our wonderful country? I say the lack of God fearing people standing up for what is good and just. Who or what is doing this to our country? Where did all the good people go? Garbage on TV and on the internet does not help. But there is much on the internet and TV that is good. It is about choices in many families. There are spiritual and supernatural entities at work.

I see very clearly, when you take God out of the picture, you are losing His protection. The USA is the greatest country in the world. We are a superpower; yet we have so many problems. For example, the fall of Rome took place after they were killing people for sport. They had no regard for human life. They took God out of their lives and declared Caesar as God. For us Christians, Jesus is the answer. Share His Love. Don't let the enemy win. This is just a little something to think about. Who is running this country called The United States of America? Do we have God fearing men and women in office? Does our President, Senate, Congress and every leader in our country use the Word of God for guidance? If not, they should. All our leaders in the past used the Bible for wisdom and guidance in making decisions to lead this Great Land. Pray for all are leaders and vote in Godly men.

"What Say You?"

Notes and comments!

Chapter 19

Bev's Faith Conquered Evil!

This is a true story of an incident that happened to one of my best friends. I am so proud of her. She did not hesitate to call on her faith in the face of tremendous danger. She is living in a beautiful sub-division on the out skirts of Tampa, Florida. This area is very beautiful and safe. Out of the blue a string of afternoon break-ins occurred that led to theft, rape and stabbing took place in and around her area. Women had been raped and stabbed with their valuables taken, all by the same man. It was a young black man and no one was able to give a description. He was fast and attacked mostly from behind. The police were at a standstill with no leads. On this one particular day Bev was babysitting her grandson. She took her grandson out for a stroller ride. She locked her entrance door to the kitchen and closed the garage door. On returning to her home with the baby still in the stroller, she opened the garage door and rolled the stroller into the garage. As she was about to open the kitchen door, she pressed the button to close the garage door. There was only about three feet left before the garage door was fully closed. Suddenly a young black man flew in under the door like a flash of lightning.

Something said to Bev, look at his face. Don't take your eyes off him. He yelled out, "Give me all your money." He was standing straight with a knife in his hand. Bev said, "I don't have any money." Then she looked him in the eye and said, "I command you to leave in the name of Jesus." The next thing that happened was he ran out faster than he arrived. I can just imagine his black Pentecostal grandmother words rushing through his thoughts as he ran.

Bev was shaking and crying with fear. Yet she was so happy at the same time that she and her grandson were safe. She called her daughter and husband and the police. She was able to give the police a very accurate description of the young man. Then they showed the photo around and someone at one of the local high schools recognized the young man. It was not a man, but just a boy in high school. They checked his attendance in school and every time one of these crimes took place, this boy was absent from school. Bev forgave the boy and has asked for all to pray for him. Bev wanted prayer for him to straighten up his life. She wanted prayers that he would be an asset to the community, not a lifetime criminal. We stand on the word of God that this boy will be the boy that God wants him to be. I believe her faith saved her and most likely the boy's too. Her angel was with her and she spoke with the authority of the Holy Spirit. The boy's guardian angel listened. The angel of darkness told him to attack and the angel of the Lord told him to leave. God Is Good!

"What say you?"

Notes and comments!

Best Friends are truly a great gift from God. In my book you read about Carol, Sheilah, Virginia & Sandy.

Thank you for reading my book. It was my pleasure to share. In His Love, Carol

I pray that you enjoy this little book and
God has blessed you. Thank you.

I ask that the reader say a prayer for my health,
Spiritual/Mentally and Physically. So I may grow
closer to God. I am truly still a work in progress.

I also ask prayers for my children and all our
children to grow strong in their faith with Jesus

Pray for thee and you shall be healed.

New Living Translation
James 5:17 ... *Confess your sins to each other*
and pray for each other so that you may be healed.
The earnest prayer of a righteous person has great
power and produces wonderful results.

Please pray for your country.
Pray for the United States of America

2 Chronicles 7:14 ... *"If my people, which are called by*
my name, shall humble themselves, and pray, and seek my
face, and turn from their wicked ways; then will I hear from
heaven, and will forgive their sin, and will heal their land."

In His Love, Carol

CPSIA information can be obtained
at www.ICGtesting.com
Printed in the USA
LVOW07s0147150817
545037LV00001B/79/P